GOOD CALL

REFLECTIONS ON FAITH, FAMILY, AND FOWL

JASE ROBERTSON

with Mark Schlabach

HOWARD BOOKS
A DIVISION OF SIMON & SCHUSTER, INC.

NEW YORK   NASHVILLE   LONDON   TORONTO   SYDNEY   NEW DELHI

Howard Books
A Division of Simon & Schuster, Inc.
1230 Avenue of the Americas
New York, NY 10020

First Howard Books hardcover edition May 2014

HOWARD and colophon are trademarks of Simon & Schuster, Inc.

For information about special discounts for bulk purchases, please contact Simon &
Schuster Special Sales at 1-866-506-1949 or business@simonandschuster.com.

The Simon & Schuster Speakers Bureau can bring authors to your live event. For
more information or to book an event, contact the Simon & Schuster Speakers
Bureau at 1-866-248-3049 or visit our website at www.simonspeakers.com.

Interior design by Jaime Putorti
Jacket design by Bruce Gore
Jacket photographs by Russell A. Graves

Manufactured in the United States of America

10 9 8 7 6 5 4 3 2 1

Library of Congress Cataloging-in-Publication Data

Robertson, Jase.
  Reflections on faith, family, and fowl / Jase Robertson With Mark Schlabach. —
First Howard Books hardcover edition.
     pages cm
1. Robertson, Jase. 2. Robertson, Jase—Family. 3. Television personalities—United
States—Biography. 4. Duck dynasty (Television program) I. Title.
  PN1992.4.R532A3 2014
  070.92—dc23
  [B]
                              2013046006

ISBN 978-1-4767-6566-2

CONTENTS

CONTENTS

ACKNOWLEDGMENTS

To my wife and best friend, Missy, who shared her heart throughout the book, thank you! Oh yeah, and for putting up with me when I became a bit grumpy from a lack of sleep. Due to my schedule, most of this book was written between midnight and five A.M.

To my kids, Reed, Cole, and Mia, for providing those moments in life when time stands still and for the contagious joy you spread to everyone around you.

To the Robertson family, who have always given me a seat at the dinner table, forgiveness, and plenty of laughs.

To my church family, who give me a place to worship with others and the encouragement to persevere in Christ.

To Mark Schlabach, for your organization skills and partnership in this book.

To Philip McMillan and Mike Williams, who helped me remember the details of stories from long ago. Thanks for always being there.

ACKNOWLEDGMENTS

To my great friend and brother in Christ Barrett Satterlee, thanks for your insight and constructive encouragement in writing this book. Convincing me to come hunting with you has been one of the best decisions I have ever made, not just because of the ducks but because it provided me a human example of godliness, family, and friendship.

To Jeremiah of the Bible, who preached about God for over forty years with seemingly no response and penned these words in Jeremiah 20:9: "But if I say, 'I will not mention him or speak any more in his name,' his word is in my heart like a fire, a fire shut up in my bones. I am weary of holding it in; indeed, I cannot."

GOOD CALL

PROLOGUE

CALL ME A QUACK

Wisdom is proved right by her actions.

—MATTHEW 11:19b

How many times have you heard the phrase "You can't judge a book by its cover"? Well, that seems to be an accurate assessment of my family. The Robertson family tends to stand out, especially in public, because of our thick beards and camouflage, but perhaps even more so because of our gorgeous wives, who accompany us without acting like they were kidnapped!

As you might know, my family has a popular TV show called *Duck Dynasty* on A&E. It might be one of the reasons you're reading my book. I believe it was our beards that caught people's attention in the beginning, but I would like to think that our sincere love for one another is what keeps people watching. Not to mention, we are unashamed of our faith in Christ and we enjoy a ton of laughs together. It has been interesting reading so many different opinions on why this show is successful. No matter the reason, we humbly appreciate the support offered by so many people.

Of course, there has been a lot of speculation over the last couple of years that our wives must have married us bearded ugly ducklings because of our fame and fortune. The fact is that none of us had much at all when we met our wives, and our long, full beards came after we married them. Our crazy uncle Si likes to joke that our gift of gab—or "hot air," as he puts it—is what helped woo our wives. Actually, our relationships were built on spiritual principles such as faith, hope, and love. Through our poverty, rugged appearances, and, at times, musty aromas, I learned that true joy doesn't come from what you have or how you look but from what kind of man you are on the inside. On my second date with Missy, I explained to her my love for hunting and fishing, which often causes me to be gone for several days and sometimes weeks at a time. I figured my admission would rule out a third date, but I was surprised when she replied, "Okay." I knew right then that Missy was a keeper, and she has become my spiritual soul mate and a wonderful mother to our three beautiful children.

One of the best things about *Duck Dynasty* is that the show allows us to be ourselves—it is *reality* TV, after all—although we don't get to film, edit, or decide what ultimately gets broadcasted on TV in the end. I like to think it's good, clean, lighthearted fun, and I don't think there's enough of that kind of entertainment in

America anymore. We realized from the start of the show that we were being afforded an incredible opportunity to have a positive impact on so many people across the country and even throughout the world. My family and I are normal people who just so happen to have some of our funny moments and mouthwatering meals together broadcast on national TV. Oh yeah, and we consistently pray together, whether the camera is on or off.

From the very beginning of *Duck Dynasty*, my family decided not to compromise our faith, to stick together no matter what, and to preserve our hunting seasons.

This has not always been easy. There have been many trials that have accompanied the notoriety that comes along with having a top-rated TV show. Perhaps the most notable revolved around comments my dad made in an interview that created national attention and quite the media frenzy. It was shocking that so many news organizations offered commentary without the knowledge of how the interview was conducted.

We have done hundreds of interviews at the request of the show and this particular event is the only one I walked out on. In fact, the entire cast left except for my dad, the interviewer, and the publicist. My dad didn't leave because the interview was conducted at his house. I asked my dad to stop the interview because the questions were hypothetical, argumentative, and controversial. But my dad has always used his home as a place to share his faith, offer love and hospitality, and answer the tough questions in people's lives.

Phil was more concerned with the interviewer as an individual person than he was with the national magazine he represented. Most people would have kicked the interviewer out for his constant foul language and controversial questions, but my dad tried to answer them and even took the man on a tour of his land.

None of us took anything personal because we know there are those opposed to Bible-based lifestyles. We considered the whole ordeal a form of spiritual warfare and it brought us even closer together as a family. But even with this controversy, our lives really haven't changed much. For whatever reason, most people assume that if your circumstances change, then your heart must change as well. Nowadays, people ask me crazy questions, like "What would you do if tragedy struck your family, or if your house burned down, or if they canceled your TV show?" My response is always the same: "Pretty much what I did yesterday, just not nearly as comfortably." That is the reason fame and fortune haven't altered the Robertson family. We consider the benefits that come from having a successful show as blessings from God to be used for something good. Second Corinthians 4:16–18 says: "Therefore we do not lose heart. Though outwardly we are wasting away, yet inwardly we are being renewed day by day . . . our light and momentary struggles are achieving for us an eternal glory . . . So we fix our eyes not on what is seen, but on what is unseen. For what is seen is temporary, but what is unseen is eternal."

I believe one of the reasons *Duck Dynasty* has been successful is the plethora of great storytellers in my family. The art of storytelling is a characteristic woven into our family heritage.

One of the most asked questions about the stories told in my family is "How much of that is true?" Of course, the answer depends on who is telling the story. There is no doubt that Uncle Si is the most entertaining storyteller among the Robertson clan. One of his most famous stories is about the time his secondhand smoke made a deer cough. The story came about after many members of my family jokingly refused to let Si hunt our deer stands because of the odor he left behind. Deer hunters know the best survival defense for a deer is his sense of smell. Si seems to think that is just a superstition and has a coughing deer story to prove it.

Even though Si has quit smoking, we encourage him to hunt his own stand with the wind blowing in his face for best results. What makes Si's stories so funny is his passion and mannerisms in telling them.

The stories I will share in this book are based on the truth to the best of my memory. My birth name is Jason Silas Robertson, and in a strange turn of events, I was actually named by my uncle Si. My dad—who I think has a guilty conscience for not witnessing my birth—has always called me Jase, and the moniker stuck. Si and I have always been close, and he has influenced my style of storytelling; however, I do try to stick to the facts. Since Uncle Si tends to stretch the truth a bit, some people assume none of my family is telling the truth when we share our past feats and accomplishments.

> One of Si's most famous stories is about the time his secondhand smoke made a deer cough.

GOOD CALL

I'll never forget the time I went duck-hunting with my buddy
Mike Williams; you'll read a lot about our adventures and she-
nanigans in this book. Mike and I were hunting blue-winged teal
ducks, which tend to move en masse, so typically you'll either
shoot your limit or not see a duck. In other words, there is a lot
of idle time involved with teal hunting, so we usually bring along
our fishing poles. After a hunt with Mike one morning, in which
we had not seen a single teal, I hooked a four-pound bass. Almost
simultaneously, one lone blue-winged teal flew over our heads. As
I was reeling in the bass, I reached for my shotgun, raised it with
only my left hand, and shot the duck. Now, I'm right-handed but
left-eye dominant. It was the first duck I ever shot left-handed,
but it would be the first of many. I eventually made the switch to
shooting left-handed permanently. It was the hardest obstacle I've
ever had to overcome in hunting, but it made me a better shot
because I'm left-eye dominant.

When Mike and I went back to my dad's house and told him
what happened, Phil didn't believe us, even though we had the teal
and bass as evidence. He'd told us about a similar feat many times
before, when his friend Hookin' Bull Thompson pulled in a fish
with one hand and shot a duck with the other. I had heard the story
many times, but only then did I realize it had now been duplicated.
No matter how many times we told Phil about what I did, he didn't
believe us. He thought we made the entire story up because of the
countless times he'd bragged about witnessing his buddy's epic feat.
Now, Mike is one of the most honest people you'll meet, so he
couldn't believe Phil thought we were lying to him.

CALL ME A QUACK

"I'm going to sign an affidavit about what you did," Mike told me. "Maybe then he'll believe us."

"Oh, drop it," I said. "That's just how my family rolls."

If you've watched enough of *Duck Dynasty*, you might actually believe Uncle Si is certifiably insane. He is actually just as crazy off camera—if not more so! Like Uncle Si says, you'd never want to be left alone with the thoughts inside his head.

Believe it or not, there was a time when a certain doctor believed I needed a psychiatric evaluation. In December 1989, shortly after the Soviets tore down the Berlin Wall, I went on a mission trip to the Ukraine with Mike Williams and Mike Kellett, who was the youth director at White's Ferry Road Church in West Monroe, Louisiana. We went to the Ukraine to distribute food and share the Gospel of Jesus. Let me tell you something, it was the hungriest I've ever been in my life. We ran out of food during the trip, mainly because the people we fed looked like they needed it a lot more than we did. I'll never forget going to the world's biggest McDonald's in Moscow on the way back home, where I ate five Happy Meals. The Happy Meals certainly made me happy, but the whole experience helped me to never take for granted how good things are in America compared to other countries.

Shortly after I returned home from the Ukraine, I became severely ill with what doctors believed was a parasite. I couldn't hold my food down and lost a lot of weight. Different doctors kept prescribing me antibiotics, but none of them seemed to help. For a couple of months, I was poked and tested in a variety of ways, only to have more questions surface than answers. Then

I was sent to an ear, nose, and throat doctor for an evaluation. I was sitting in a waiting room with a bunch of toddlers, when my name was called. By the time I got into the examination room, I knew I'd had enough.

"Hey, I'm outta here," I told the doctor. "I'll take my chances with the resurrection."

Well, a couple of weeks later, my insurance agent called me. He was one of my lifelong friends and sounded concerned.

"Hey, Jase," he said. "Your insurance company wants you to see a psychiatrist."

Apparently, the ear, nose, and throat doctor recommended I undergo a full psychiatric evaluation based on my refusal to be examined, along with my speech on the resurrection! Apparently, he thought I was crazy. I convinced my buddy that I didn't need a psychiatrist and eventually got over my illness. I would later read a passage of scripture in the Bible that caused me to smile in reflection on the entire ordeal. Second Corinthians 5:13 says: "If we are out of our mind, as some say, it is for God; if we are in our right mind, it is for you."

Most people view me on *Duck Dynasty* as a bit of a "goofball" or someone who is extremely sarcastic (which is true) and who would rather hunt and fish than go to work (absolutely true). However, I hope that by reading this book, you discover that my carefree attitude and joy for life come from what I have found in Jesus Christ. My favorite verse from the Bible is Hebrews 13:8:

> "Hey, Jase," he said. "Your insurance company wants you to see a psychiatrist."

"Jesus Christ is the same yesterday and today and forever." If Jesus is Lord of life and death, then it's about Him and certainly not about me or us as individuals. Who He is, what He did for humanity, and what He will do in heaven trumps whatever it is I think I can offer on my own while here on the earth. Through Jesus, your past is explained, your present has a purpose, and your future is secure. What more could you really want in life?

The Robertsons' goal was never to be known as TV stars (except maybe Uncle Si, but, hey, he's nuts—in a good way). In fact, I wasn't even convinced the show would actually happen until I looked out my window one morning and saw cameramen running through my brother Willie's front yard like bees swarming to a hive. I'll never forget overhearing what one of the cameramen whispered to a technician on the first day of filming. He was sad that the show would probably tear our family apart. I remember thinking to myself, *He hasn't met my family.* He didn't know that the only kind of stardom my family and I are interested in is the lifestyle in Christ as described in Philippians 2:15–16: "Children of God . . . [that] shine like stars in the universe as you hold out the word of life." One thing my family has always done is treat every living person with love and respect, regardless of race, faults, circumstances, or beliefs. When my brothers and I were growing up on the Ouachita River in West Monroe, we were known as "river rats" and "rednecks" because we didn't have much in terms of money or material possessions. However, our home was always open and our goal was to share by word or deed what we found in Jesus Christ as Lord.

I've enjoyed working with my hands building duck calls for more than thirty years to make an earthly living for my family, but introducing God to other people brings me a joy that is priceless. I'm far from perfect, and I'm certainly not a preacher who works for a particular religious denomination or supports an agenda outside of God, Jesus Christ, the Holy Spirit, and the Bible. I'm not a theologian, nor do I claim to be an expert in anything—well, maybe except for sounding like a duck.

You can call me a quack, and you'd be right on target.

1

FORGIVING PHIL

MAKING PEACE WITH THE PAST

A man's wisdom gives him patience;
it is to his glory to overlook an offense.

—PROVERBS 19:11

By now, you might know the story of my dad's life. If you haven't heard it or read about it, here's the most blunt way I can describe it: Phil Robertson wasn't a very nice person from about the age of seventeen until he turned twenty-eight. In a lot of ways, my dad was an outlaw. He had no regard for rules, authority, or what was right or wrong; his only focus at the time was getting drunk and killing as many ducks as possible. And anyone standing in his way, even his own family, ran the risk of getting hurt.

Don't get me wrong; Phil Robertson eventually became a great husband, father, and businessman, and, most important, a disciple of Christ. After my dad's repentance, he became the biggest influence in my life because of his love for his Creator, hunting and fishing, and nurturing God's greatest creation. Once my dad turned from his wicked ways and submitted to Jesus Christ as his Lord and Savior, he became a role model for people struggling to overcome their addictions and problems. It wasn't so much that he focused on their problems but that he offered them a solution. His life wasn't easy when he was drinking, partying, and committing other sins, and it certainly was difficult for the people who loved him most. But once my dad turned his life around, he made a profound impact on thousands of people by sharing God's story of healing and hope. He became a man of faith, perseverance, and courage. But the decade or so before his baptism wasn't easy for my mom or me and my brothers.

My recollections of my childhood are kind of hazy, which might be a good thing, because I don't have many fond memories of growing up until my father was born again; his becoming a new man is the most drastic change in a person I have ever seen. I remember my family owning a bar in Junction City, Arkansas, for a couple of years, and it seemed like every night ended with men rolling around on the ground and fighting, followed by flashing lights from police cars in the parking lot.

> Most every night ended with men rolling around the ground and fighting, followed by flashing lights from police cars in the parking lot.

It also seemed that no matter what, my dad usually won the fight. I remember one particular fight outside the bar, when an Asian-looking man grabbed a board. The man was doing all of these martial arts moves complete with sound effects, and all of a sudden he swung the board at my dad. In the blink of an eye, my dad grabbed the board out of his hands and popped him in the head with it! The guy fell like a sack of potatoes.

My family lost the bar after my dad beat up the couple who owned the building after they'd had a dispute about rent. Phil hurt them pretty badly, and he fled into the swamp to avoid getting arrested. The people my dad beat up took about everything we had; in exchange they agreed not to press criminal charges against him. My mom moved our trailer near D'Arbonne Lake at Farmerville, Louisiana, and I was forced to change schools again. We moved a lot when I was a kid, and there never seemed to be much stability in our lives.

After the fight at the bar, my dad was gone for several months. I remember going to visit him in the woods one time, and when we pulled up he was drinking beer with two of his buddies. They were living in a hut that didn't even have electricity or running water. There was a massive pile of empty beer cans and liquor bottles. There was also a big pile of animal carcasses. It was unbelievable. As a kid, I'd never seen anything like it before. I remember getting out of the vehicle thinking, *How long has my dad been out here?* He was walking around barefoot. Of course, as his impressionable son, I thought he was the toughest man in the world because he was living in those conditions.

My dad walked up to me and asked, "How's it going?" We had a normal conversation right there in the middle of nowhere. This might sound crazy, but as I look back at the experience now, I think it taught me that a person is capable of living in the woods and surviving without the luxuries we have today. I probably realized then that I wanted to spend most of my life in the woods or on the water.

My dad eventually moved back into the trailer with us, but he didn't stop drinking. In fact, it only got worse. He often took out his anger on my mom, my brothers, and me, and even though I was young, I understood that it was the beer and liquor making him so mean. I feared being around him. I think my dad tried to quit drinking more than a few times, but alcohol always seemed to get the best of him. One night, while Phil was driving home from a hunt, he threw a half-empty liquor bottle out the window of his truck. I guess he finally decided it was time to stop drinking. But a few hours later, my dad had my brothers and me on the side of the road in the dark, searching a ditch for his liquor bottle. What might seem like terrible parenting was actually one of my first adventures in hunting. I found my dad's bottle, so I figured I would one day make a pretty good tracker in the woods.

In a lot of ways, my dad's behavior made me shy and introverted, which is something I struggled with until I was a teenager. I never said much as a kid around my dad. I was afraid that if I did say something, I would get in trouble. It didn't take me long to figure out that as long as I was out of his sight and didn't say anything, I could pretty much stay out of harm's way. I kept my mouth shut to survive, and I went into a cocoon as a kid because of my circumstances. I was kind of antisocial until high

> A few hours later, my dad had my brothers and me on the side of the road in the dark, searching a ditch for his liquor bottle.

school, but then I realized I would have to be more vocal if I wanted to share my faith or get a date.

Perhaps the most vivid memory I have of my early childhood is the night my dad kicked us out of our trailer. I was about seven years old at the time. I remember seeing my dad stretched out on the couch with a tall can of beer between his legs as we gathered our belongings in the middle of the night. We headed out the front door, not knowing when or if we would ever see him again. My mother was in tears and pleaded with him to let us stay, but he wouldn't change his mind. He kept yelling at Kay to leave. I had no idea where she was taking my older brother, Alan; my younger brother, Willie; and me. We didn't have any money, so it wasn't like we were going to go stay in a hotel for a couple of weeks. We spent the night at my uncle Harold's house, and then we moved into a low-rent apartment in West Monroe, Louisiana. White's Ferry Road Church in West Monroe helped us get furniture and assisted my mother in paying the rent.

Our move to the apartment complex is a foggy memory, but it seemed a lot more stable and safe than the place we left. My mom took a job at Howard Brothers Discount Stores, working in the corporate office, so Alan was left to take care of Willie and me when we weren't in school. I didn't see my father for a long time. I was bitter about it, too. No matter how mean your parents are or what they're doing to you, as a kid they're all you have, and that's the way it is, for better or worse. Even though my dad wasn't a nice person to be around, I couldn't understand why in the world he would abandon his family. My dad's reason for his path of ruin and misery during his first twenty-eight years on earth was that he just wanted to "be free." Apparently, that meant leaving his wife and children behind so he could hunt, fish, and drink whenever he wanted.

About the time I finally stopped wondering where my dad was, he showed up in a cool green Jeep outside of our apartment building. Earlier that day, he had driven to my mom's office, and she found him crying in the parking lot. Phil begged her to take him back, and fortunately my mom found enough compassion and love in her heart to forgive him. She told him he had to stop drinking and disassociate himself from his unsavory friends. My dad met with William "Bill" Smith, the preacher at White's Ferry Road Church. My dad studied the Bible with him and was introduced to Jesus Christ for the first time. After a couple of studies and a lot of soul-searching, my dad made a decision to repent and claim Christ as Lord, and he was baptized. Romans 6:1–4 discusses baptism as a reenactment of Jesus' death, burial, and resurrection. The burial of the old Phil Robertson and the rebirth of the new man who surfaced was one of the most powerful influences of my life. I'm sure there were still plenty of rough times for him as he battled temptations over the next couple of years, but my brothers and I were happy our dad was back in our lives.

My dad really got my attention during our first Christmas back together as a family again. He participated in the giving of gifts, and, more important, played the games we had received with us. He was turning into the father we had always wanted him to be. Looking back, it's amazing that kids are so forgiving, because they really don't understand all the details of what's going on. They're so innocent and naive. Despite everything that had happened in the past, I was happy my dad was finally paying attention to my brothers and me. That's really the only thing we ever wanted from him. We were going to church a couple of times a week, and my mom seemed so happy that our family was together. I would love to say that my new church experience had a big impact on my life at the time, but it was uncomfortable for me to be around so many strangers. Honestly, it seemed like a bigger version of the honky-tonk bar, but without all of the hollering and fighting.

> Despite everything that had happened in the past, I was happy my dad was finally paying attention to my brothers and me.

After my dad got his life back in order, he took a teaching job at Ouachita Christian School in Monroe, Louisiana. He'd attended Louisiana Tech University on a football scholarship and earned a master's degree in education. Even though he wasn't drinking anymore, he still loved to hunt and fish and wanted to spend as much time as possible in the outdoors, so he decided to quit his teaching job and do something that allowed him to hunt and fish. We moved to a house on the banks of the Ouachita River, which is about twenty-five miles from downtown West Monroe. My dad started working as a commercial fisherman, and then he started building duck calls because he was convinced he could make a call sound more like a duck than anyone else in the world. He was right.

Shortly after we moved closer to the river, my dad and a few of his friends started a church in Luna, Louisiana. It was a small church of about forty members, and I didn't really like going to services there because there weren't many kids my age. One Sunday morning, my dad went to the pulpit and gave his testimony. It was entitled, "The Good News and the Bad News." Of course, I was in attendance, but I wasn't really paying attention to what he was saying. I was astounded that he was acting nervous. I'd never seen the man nervous in my life! I always believed he was the most self-confident man in the world.

One of my friends, Matt, who was a couple of years older than me, was sitting next to me in church. He apparently was very moved by my dad's sermon. My friend and I had a discussion about the Gospel, and it kind of broke the ice for faith in Christ being a reality in my life. Up until that time, I'd thought about what it meant to be a Christian, but I hadn't taken the step for myself. I remember riding in the car with my mom going to school one morning. We stopped at a red light in front of the paper mill in West Monroe, and she asked me, "Are you going to be a Christian when you grow up?" Now, I'm not a morning person unless I'm going hunting, so I was kind of annoyed by her question. I don't like to be interrogated when I'm still waking up. I stared out the window and thought, *Well, am I, or am I not?*

"Yes, ma'am, I believe I am," I told her.

Even though I waited a couple of years to do it, I think my mom's question planted the seed for my conversion. After my conversation with Matt, I went to my dad to talk about it. I told him what I had come to understand about Christ, and he said,

"Well, that's what I heard. What you're thinking about doing is what changed my life."

"Well, sir," I said, "I'm ready to do it."

We walked to the riverbank, and my dad baptized me in the Ouachita River, which is where we've baptized hundreds of people over the years. Right then and there, I decided I was going to forgive my father for everything that happened in the past. The past was history, and I was excited about our future together as Christian men. My father had given me the greatest gift in life. How could I not forgive him?

As I reflect back on my dad's pre-Christ life, I realize that by embracing the Son of God, who died on a cross for his mistakes, my dad was given a second chance and a life of continual forgiveness. I came to realize that same cross is where I would find forgiveness. My life has never included drugs or drunkenness, mainly because I saw what they did to my dad and our family. But as my dad once said, "You're either a rank heathen like I was or just a heathen." I have made my share of mistakes and realize that a life without forgiveness is a life filled with guilt, bitterness, and misery no matter how many sins you've committed or which ones they are. Once I became a Christian, I viewed being part of the forgiven as synonymous with being a

> I learned to forgive my dad for his mistakes. It was a huge step for me.

forgiver. I learned to forgive my dad for his mistakes. It was a huge step for me, but it's impossible to find harmony in relationships when there is no forgiveness. After all, everyone make mistakes and no one is perfect.

Later in life, my wife, Missy, and I shared God's message of grace with a single mother who had a gut-wrenching story of a lifetime of physical, mental, and sexual abuse. If there was ever a person who had a reason to quit in life, or at least retaliate toward her abusers, this woman was it. Her tears flowed as Missy and I shared the story of Jesus. To my surprise, she was not only moved by God's love for her but she also even found a place for the sins committed by those people who abused her—a bloody cross. I was almost uncomfortable with her response because she was willing to forgive the people who had tormented her for so long. She became one of my heroes because of her grace and compassion.

I have a special place in my heart for those who are sinned against, and while I believe we should do everything in our power to protect the innocent and punish the guilty on earth, there is something special about the people who overcome atrocities through grace and forgiveness because of a loving God in heaven. I suppose the most common argument against the evidence for God is, "Why do bad things happen to good people?" It is a valid question, but it is a question the Gospel—Jesus' life, death, burial, resurrection, and return—answers for us. If we can obtain forgiveness in this life and eternity in the next, all other things really do not matter. The Parable of the Unmerciful Servant from Matthew 18:21–35 has always had a profound effect on me and taught me a lot about forgiveness:

Then Peter came to Jesus and asked, "Lord, how many times shall I forgive my brother when he sins against me? Up to seven times?"

Jesus answered, "I tell you, not seven times, but seventy-seven times.

"Therefore, the kingdom of heaven is like a king who wanted to settle accounts with his servants. As he began the settlement, a man who owed him ten thousand talents was brought to him. Since he was not able to pay, the master ordered that he and his wife and his children and all that he had be sold to repay the debt.

"The servant fell on his knees before him. 'Be patient with me,' he begged, 'and I will pay back everything.' The servant's master took pity on him, canceled the debt and let him go.

"But when that servant went out, he found one of his fellow servants who owed him a hundred denarii. He grabbed him and began to choke him. 'Pay back what you owe me!' he demanded.

"His fellow servant fell to his knees and begged him, 'Be patient with me, and I will pay you back.'

"But he refused. Instead, he went off and had the man thrown into prison until he could pay the debt. When the other servants saw what had happened, they were greatly distressed and went and told their master everything that had happened.

"Then the master called the servant in. 'You wicked servant,' he said, 'I canceled all that debt of yours because you begged me to. Shouldn't you have had mercy on your fellow servant just as I had on you?' In anger his master turned him over to the jailers to be tortured, until he should pay back all he owed.

GOOD CALL

*"This is how my heavenly Father will treat each of you
unless you forgive your brother from your heart."*

What I've learned from this scripture is that we need to have mercy and forgive one another, as God is merciful in forgiving us. Forgiveness cannot be based on the quantity or consequences of sins. You're either with or without sin, and our God-given conscience confirms our guilt. Christ is without sin and that is why His death was God's justice, mercy, and forgiveness in action. When we have unforgiving hearts, we are like the unforgiving servant. God's forgiveness of our sins should motivate us to forgive those who offend us. My motivation to forgive is my own forgiveness. I can never repay God what I owe. Christ paid for our sins by dying on the cross, and we can never repay that debt.

As I have observed my dad's post-Christ life, I have seen a man who has been open and honest about his past mistakes. His blunt speech about sin is a powerful testimony of the transformation that God's grace offers, but it also is a target of those who are uncomfortable with Bible-based faith. Fortunately, for my family and those in earshot of my dad's voice, he has almost forty years of righteous actions that show a humble walk with God and an unselfish love for all people regardless of their circumstances in life. To those in opposition to God's grace and a righteous lifestyle, Jesus said it best, "Father, forgive them, for they do not know what they are doing."

FAMILY TIES

BIRDS OF A FEATHER FLOCK TOGETHER

A man of many companions may come to ruin, but
there is a friend who sticks closer than a brother.
—PROVERBS 18:24

After my dad became a disciple of Jesus Christ, it was really amazing to see how much our lives changed. He was a completely different person, and we were almost like an entirely new family. When I was around eight years old, I remember being crammed in a truck with my parents, two brothers, and a real estate agent, who was taking us to see a piece of property on the Ouachita River outside of West Monroe, Louisiana. As soon as our truck topped a sizable hill before the last curve to our destination, we saw a majestic view of the rolling river.

My dad uncontrollably blurted out, "We'll take it!"

My mom immediately responded with a gasp and then an elbow to his side. We hadn't even seen the two houses for sale, nor the seven acres of land that came with them! But it didn't matter to my dad, and quite frankly, I agreed with him. As far as we were concerned, the land was perfect, because it was so close to the river. I'm sure my dad was daydreaming about the duck hunting and fishing the land would afford us—just like I was—as we pulled up to the property. Examining the condition of the houses was simply a formality, as was negotiating a price with the Realtor, because of my dad's excitement.

After we parked our truck, my dad marched into the empty house that would become my parents' home for the next thirty-five years—and is still their house today. He promptly turned on the only luxury available—an old wall-mounted air-conditioning unit—and sprawled out in the middle of the dusty floor. A feeling of freedom seemed to ooze out of his pores as he lay in his newly found paradise, and he was grinning from ear to ear. It was like he was telling me, "We've hit the big time here, son." I'd never seen my dad so happy.

Even at such a young age, I could sense that things were different. I'd just been reintroduced to my new born-again father, and I felt the fear and chaos of my childhood had somehow taken a turn for the better. Sure, there were a few hiccups along the way, but my father was a changed man. The move to the Ouachita River was the biggest moment of my life because it reconnected me to my father through hunting and fishing. I took up hunting and fishing more than my brothers, so I think there was even more of a connection

> A feeling of freedom seemed to ooze out of his pores as he lay in his newly found paradise.

between my dad and me. I was his right-hand man in the commercial fishing business and making duck calls. Most of the time when we were in the boat, it was just my dad and me.

Now, you have to understand this: I've always viewed my parents more as friends than actual parents. I know all of the self-help parenting books tell us you're not supposed to be "friends" with your children because it skews their perception of authority and obedience, but my parents were my best friends. I mean, that's just the way I looked at it, and that's probably one of the primary reasons my brothers and I have always called them by their first names. Another reason we call them Phil and Kay is that when we were operating Duck Commander out of our house, we wanted to keep telephone calls with customers somewhat professional, so we were taught to never call them Mom and Dad when talking on the phone. We would often say, "Phil, line one," to sound professional. Of course, we only had one line, but it just sounded better than, "Hold on, let me get my dad."

Once we moved to the river, I started to learn about Phil Robertson the man. There's no doubt his most dominant physical feature is his beard. Over the years, it became a symbol of his independence and carefree living.

When I helped my dad in the commercial fishing business, I didn't view it as work because I loved doing it so much. Don't get me wrong; it was backbreaking work, especially for a young boy. But I learned a lot of valuable lessons about hard work on the river. I knew what every fish was worth. A catfish brought seventy cents per pound at market, buffalo was worth thirty cents per pound, and gar was twenty cents per pound. My excitement came from figuring out how much money we made from fishing every day, but I had no use for the actual money. We were living in the middle of nowhere. What was I going to do with it? Our hunting and fishing provided us what we needed to eat, and my dad took care of everything we needed for hunting. Really, I didn't have a care in the world.

Over the years, my dad taught me the skill of fishing, such as finding the underwater highways fish traveled the most and how to use nets to catch them. The science of fishing has always intrigued me, and it's the same attraction for me in hunting.

The amount of fish we caught literally determined what we ate for supper and how much gas went into our vehicle. The biggest problem we faced was people stealing our nets and fish. Sometimes the thieves would ruin the nets by cutting the fish out. The first time it happened, I asked my dad if we should call the police, but he said, "Son, where we live, I am 911." He policed the river and would awaken many times during the night to check out boats he heard motoring by. I was with him during a few confrontations after we caught people in the act of stealing our nets. They were the most intense moments of my childhood. How my dad handled these situations was in a way a reflection of his growth as a Christian. He started out with a shotgun and a threat to use it if he ever caught them stealing again. But then one day when we caught two guys red-handed, Dad raised his

> The science of fishing has always intrigued me, and it's the same attraction for me in hunting.

shotgun and gave one of the best sermons from the Bible I've ever heard. Toward the end of our commercial-fishing career, he would have the gun but not raise it, give the sermon, and then give them the fish. He would tell them, "If you wanted some fish, all you had to do was ask." I actually saw grown men shed tears over this approach, and a couple of them came to the Lord.

Fishing the river wasn't easy. During the summertime, when there wasn't a current on the Ouachita River, we'd use trammel nets to fish, and it was really hard work. A trammel net is like a ten-foot wall stretching across the river. There are floats on top of the net and weights on the bottom. Of course, there's netting in the middle. When fish go through the outlying walls of the netting, they immediately turn to the right or the left and get tangled in the webbing. We'd put about six or seven trammel nets at various spots along the river. The nets were one hundred fifty yards long, and we'd space them a few hundred yards apart. We'd put them out in the evening and then run them in the morning, taking whatever fish we caught to market. We'd run them again in the evening and put whatever fish we caught on ice. We did it over and over again every day in the summer. It might seem like tedious work to some people, but I wouldn't have traded the job for anything in the world. It was one of the most exciting times of my life.

When you're using trammel nets to fish, you can get pretty far from home on the river. After a couple of months, you're many miles up the river. You keep moving, looking for fish. I remember running the nets one morning, and I was wearing only a pair of shorts.

I rarely wore socks, shoes, or a shirt during the summertime fishing period. We didn't have a lot of clothes when I was growing up, and I didn't want my entire wardrobe smelling like fish! On this particular day, a big thunderstorm came through, and it poured. Of course, there was nowhere to hide on the river and we were too far from home to get back. When the storm finally passed, I was freezing. It seemed like the temperature had dropped thirty degrees! When we started motoring back to our house, the wind made it even colder.

Usually, my dad is all about "Who's a man?" and "How tough are you?" But all of a sudden, he slowed down the motor and stopped.

"You know what?" he asked me. "I'm freezing my rear off."

"I'm pretty cold, too," I told him as my teeth chattered.

"I've got an idea," he said.

"What's that?" I asked him.

"Feel the water," he said.

I put my hand in the river and it felt like bathwater. My dad and I jumped into the river and drifted home as we held on to the boat. We talked and laughed the entire way home. I don't know why I've always remembered that experience; I guess it's because my dad turned a miserable incident into a good memory for me. For once, it wasn't about toughness and being a man. One of the greatest things about hunting and fishing as a kid is you're spending quality time with your parents and probably don't even realize it at the time.

Whenever it rained, we always made sure to check the beaver dams on the river. After it rains, game fish like to gather up where the current comes across the dams. We usually threw a couple of rods and reels in the boat on rainy days. I remember one particular morning we pulled up to a flooded beaver dam and caught over a hundred largemouth bass. We were cack-

> My dad turned a miserable incident into a good memory for me. For once, it wasn't about toughness and being a man.

ling like little girls at a slumber party. On the way back we also caught the biggest fish I've ever seen out of a trammel net. My dad caught a seven-foot gar that weighed about one hundred and forty-five pounds! It was a giant! It was a monster! We went home and my dad immediately called the guy who bought our fish. He sold the gar for about thirty dollars. It always struck me that the fish might have eaten me if I'd fallen in the water. That's one of the great things about fishing—you never know what you're going to catch!

My dad didn't allow us to fool around in the boat or in a duck blind. It was too dangerous. He only had a few rules: my brothers and I couldn't physically fight with one another, we had to take care of our fishing and hunting equipment, and we'd better not talk back to our mother. His blood would boil if one of us broke a fishing pole or motor because of carelessness. Eventually, he trusted me enough to let me fish the river on my own.

After my dad started making duck calls, he'd leave town for a few days, driving all over Louisiana, Arkansas, Mississippi, and Texas trying to sell them. He left me in charge of the fishing operation. I was only a teenager, but it was my responsibility to check almost eighty hoop nets three times a week. Looking back now, it was pretty dangerous work for a teenager on the river, especially since I'd never done it alone. If you fell out of the boat and into the river, chances were you might drown if something went wrong and you were alone. But I was determined to prove to my father that I could do it, so I left the house one morning and spent all day on the river. I checked every one of our hoop nets and brought a mound of fish back to Kay to take to market. I was so proud of myself for pulling it off without anyone's help!

When Dad came home a couple of days later, Mom told him about the fish I'd caught and how much money we'd made. I could see the smile on his face. But then he went outside to check his boat and noticed that a paddle was missing. Instead of saying, "Good job, son," he yelled at me for losing a paddle! I couldn't believe he was scolding me over a stupid oar! I'd worked from daylight to dusk and earned enough money for my family to buy a dozen paddles! Where was the gratitude?

I was so mad that I jumped in the boat and headed to the nets to see if I could find the missing paddle. After checking about seventy nets, I was resigned to the fact that it was probably gone. But when I finally reached the seventy-ninth net, I saw the paddle lying in a few bushes where I'd tied up a headliner, which is a rope leading to the net. It was almost like a religious experience for me. What were the odds of my finding a lost paddle floating in a current on a washed-out river? It was like looking for a needle in a haystack. I took the paddle back to my dad, but he was still mad

> I finally concluded that everyone has quirks, and apparently my dad has some sort of weird love affair with boat paddles.

at me for losing it in the first place. I have never liked the line "up a creek without a paddle" because of the trouble boat paddles caused me. I swore I would never lose another one, but lo and behold, the next year, I broke the same paddle I'd lost while trying to kill a cottonmouth water moccasin that almost bit me. My dad wasn't very compassionate even after I told him his prized paddle perhaps saved my life. I finally concluded that everyone has quirks, and apparently my dad has some sort of weird love affair with boat paddles.

I started dating Missy shortly after I'd graduated from high school. She couldn't understand why I was working so hard for my parents without receiving much of a salary in return.

Missy: After a few dates, I realized he didn't have a job and wasn't going to school. I was busy being a junior in high school and planning my time as a college student in the near future, so this seemed very odd to me. It didn't take me long to figure out that while I was at school during the day, he was fishing on the river, mending nets, working crawfish traps on his dad's land, and not receiving any kind of a paycheck. I knew he was a smart guy, so I couldn't figure out why he wasn't pursuing more in his life during this time. So one day, I finally asked him, "Why are you working so hard every day when you know you're not going to get any money from it?" He said simply, "Because my parents need me." I remember feeling in awe of the loyalty Jase felt toward his parents. Those were difficult times finan-cially for them, and Jase understood, even at the wise old age of nineteen, that it would take his efforts to help Phil and Kay make ends meet. In return, Jase received three meals a day (awesome meals for sure), a bed, and even a little gas money to take me on dates. He was perfectly happy with the situation. I knew right then I had a good man on my hands.

Once during that first year of dating, I was sitting in the Robertson living room when Miss Kay came stomping in from the back room telling Willie that his room was a mess. She couldn't even get to the washing machine to do the laundry (Willie had his bed in the laundry room/pantry at that time). Without even looking at her, Willie said, "I'll clean it for five dollars." I remember laughing, thinking he was joking, especially when his brother had been outside working on the nets all day. But do you know? She actually paid him. Even back then, Willie was showing signs of being a shrewd businessman.

If I wasn't hunting and fishing with my dad when I was a kid, I was usually spending time with my grandparents Merritt and James Robertson, who lived in a second house on our land. We called them Granny and Pa. My grandfather worked on oil rigs for a long time. After Pa retired, they moved back to Louisiana from Arizona and helped my parents buy the property on the Ouachita River. Pa liked to hunt and fish and helped my dad make duck calls in the early days of Duck Commander. But as my grandparents got older, they liked to watch TV and play games with my brothers and me.

Pa and Granny were really two of my best friends growing up. They loved to tell jokes. If my dad was working or my mom was cooking, my grandparents entertained us. They never complained about it and loved the company. Our favorite games were dominoes and spades. We played cards or dominoes every day, and I became very good at them. Later in life, after the proliferation of computers, I started playing a spades game called Ladders on the Internet. When I signed up, I was ranked like 250,000th in the world. I eventually made it to number one in the world because I played it so much!

I still consider myself a professional card and dominoes player, and I warn my friends not to sit to my right or left. It's a joke meant to convey to them that my teammate sits across from me, but I find most people take it as a challenge. I became a very good poker player, and when Missy and I were first married, I played in a lot of poker games to make money. You gauge your success at poker in the long term, and I've never had a year when I didn't come out ahead, way ahead. Hey, it's not gambling if you know you're going to win, right? That's just the honest truth. I do not consider myself a gambler, as I never play blackjack or other games of chance because the odds aren't in your favor. I prefer Texas Hold'em poker or other card games in which you create your own odds by the way you play. You're not playing against a casino in poker; you're playing against other people. I consider it a game of skill in which some luck is involved. In the end, the best player is going to win. I view poker a lot like the fishing tournaments I used to participate in. You can be the best overall fisher-

GOOD CALL

> There was a day when I depended on playing cards for my spending money.

man but on any given day have bad luck. But over the long haul your skill wins out. When I play cards with my buddies now, the stakes are low and it's more about good fun than winning or losing. But there was a day when I depended on playing cards for my spending money.

Granny and Pa were great dominoes players, and our games were fierce competitions. I think outsiders were surprised at how intense the games became. Missy was shocked the first time she witnessed a Robertson family dominoes game.

Missy: The first time I met Granny and Pa was at their house during a dominoes game. Phil, Jase, Willie, and Alan were all playing with Granny and Pa at their living room table. When I arrived, I heard all kinds of banging and slamming noises. I thought someone was tearing the room apart! When I got inside, it looked like a pool hall. Granny and Pa both smoked cigarettes, and the smoke was so thick that you could cut it with a knife. Through the smoke I saw all of them slamming down domino after domino onto the wooden table and yelling at one another. I was appalled, thinking how disrespectful the boys were being to their dad and grandparents! Jase introduced me to Granny and Pa, and in between puffs, I received a polite smile from Granny and a nod from Pa. Then they went right back to yelling and slamming. Since I'd never been around smokers, I couldn't stay there for more than a few minutes. I told Jase I would be next door at his house, waiting on him to finish playing. When he finally came home, I asked him if everything was okay between everyone over there. Realizing my genuine concern, he said, "Hey, that's just part of the game." See, to them, it was only a friendly game of dominoes. I learned quickly how close Jase was to his family. It was an almost-nightly occurrence. It was hard for me to relate because I had never lived that close to my grandparents or had that kind of daily relationship with any of them. Jase and his brothers showed a comfort with their granny and pa that I had never experienced in my own life. The more time I spent with them, the more I came to love them. Pa was always very quiet and reserved (unless he had dominoes in his hands). They became very special people in my life as well.

Granny had health problems throughout her life and was even hospitalized in the Louisiana state mental institute for a while. Once doctors administered her the right kind of medicine, she had a very productive and fruitful life. She loved being around her grandchildren. One of the best things Granny did for our family was knit each of us an afghan. At some point in her life, she knitted an afghan for every one of her children and grandchildren for a special occasion. If she wasn't playing dominoes or cards, she was usually knitting in her chair. She knew I was a big Louisiana State University football fan, so she made me a big purple, gold, and white one (the Tigers' school colors) and gave it to Missy and me on our wedding day. She gave it to me twenty-five years ago, and it's still one of my most prized possessions. Granny also made each of my three children an afghan blanket. Mia, who is ten at the time of this writing, still sleeps with her afghan, or at least what's left of it. Granny's afghans are masterpieces as far as I'm concerned, not as much for the way they look but because she put so much hard work and love into making each one of them.

In a lot of ways, my family is knitted together, just like one of Granny's afghans. There were plenty of times my family might have come apart at the seams, especially when my dad was running wild. But once he followed my mother's lead and became a disciple of Christ, everything changed. My parents never pressured my brothers or me to become Christians. They realized it was a personal choice each of us had to make on his own. But our mutual love for God and one another is what kept my family intact.

One Sunday, I was asked to speak in front of our congregation at White's Ferry Road Church in West Monroe. I was asked to talk about my heroes. I'm sure everyone assumed I'd talk about my dad because he's accomplished so much in life and served as a role model for people who want to turn their lives around. Instead, I told my family and friends that my mom is my biggest hero. Even though my parents weren't Christians when I was a young kid, she put enough godly influence in us to teach us what was right and wrong. She was the glue that held everything together during the hard times. If she wasn't determined to keep her family together, our family might have dissolved. It took a lot of patience and love to keep us somewhat secure and stable despite all the chaos. I still remember the tears

> My parents never pressured my brothers or me to become Christians. They realized it was a personal choice each of us had to make on his own.

flowing down her cheeks after I spoke, and as only my mom can, she cooked all my favorite meals for the next week.

My childhood was marked by the transformation of my parents and our move to the riverbank. My wife, Missy, and I watched the movie *Mud* last year. It stars Matthew McConaughey as a fugitive living in a broken-down boat on an island in the Arkansas delta. He enlists two young boys to help him renovate the boat so he can use it to skip town. As we were watching the movie, Missy confessed to me that she'd never considered that some people actually choose to live a simple life, like my family did along the Ouachita River. It didn't help when I confessed to her that if someone had offered me a million-dollar house in the city when I was a kid, I would have turned it down. Once we moved to the banks of the Ouachita River, I wouldn't have traded my childhood for anything.

FIRST HUNT

INHERITING PHIL'S PASSION FOR THE CHASE

The earth is the Lord's, and everything in it, the world,
and all who live in it; for he founded it upon the seas
and established it upon the waters.

—PSALM 24:1–2

About a year after we moved to the banks of the Ouachita River, my dad took me on my first duck hunt. I was about eight years old, and it turned out to be a monumental moment in my life. That morning, my dad woke me from a dead sleep with words he would eventually utter hundreds of times in the future: "Hey, Jase, you ready? You ready? Jase, you ready?" He told me later that he kept asking me if I was ready until he finally received a big grin from me. One thing I have learned about myself is that I'm always ready to hunt or fish no matter the circumstance.

On the morning of my first hunt, I remember trying to stay awake as we drove on and on for what seemed to be forever. We stopped at an old convenience store, and it seemed strange to see so much human activity that early in the morning. Like I said earlier, I'm not a morning person unless I'm going hunting. I'd never been awake at four o'clock in the morning until my very first hunt. It was so dark, and I felt sick to my stomach. Maybe it was my nerves, or just the fact that I wasn't used to being up so early, but I learned later that many members of the Robertson family are notoriously susceptible to motion sickness in a variety of settings.

As we continued to drive to the duck blind, my dad cracked the window of his truck and gave me stern directions: "If you gotta throw up, stick your head out the window, and I'll give it some gas." By the time we made it to the Arkansas state line, I was lying in the fetal position in the bed of his truck. I felt terrible. I could see mud flying up on both sides of the truck. I remember thinking that if I had to lean over the side of his truck to throw up, I was going to get very muddy. The conversation I overheard between my dad and his hunting buddies didn't make me feel much better, either.

Al Bolen, one of my dad's best friends, told him, "I can't believe you're going to let Jase shoot that Magnum Twelve. It's going to stomp him into the ground!"

"Well, he is good for a limit anyway," my dad said.

> "If you gotta throw up, stick your head out the window, and I'll give it some gas."

I had no idea what my dad was talking about, but later I would come to understand that duck limits are calculated on an individual basis. The more hunters you have in the blind, the more ducks you're allowed to kill. My dad had definitely changed, but he was still having difficulty communicating his newly found faith to his old buddies. I think he really wanted to take me hunting, but he was still trying to convey the toughness his old drinking buddies expected from him. To be honest, I was so happy to be going hunting with my dad, I didn't care if I was only going for the limit. I was much more concerned about what Mr. Al said about the shotgun stomping me into the ground.

The next thing I knew I was being ordered into a boat, and then we motored through pitch-black darkness. It baffled me that no one was shining a light to see where we were headed, and nobody seemed uncomfortable with the darkness. I didn't know at the time that the best way to enter a swamp when you are scouting or hunting is to do so stealthily. A true hunter uses his memory, his instincts, and the silhouettes of the swamp for navigation in the dark. After several minutes, we arrived at a very big tree. It was the biggest cypress tree I'd ever seen! I was shocked when Mr. Al shined a light up the hollowed-out trunk of the tree and said, "All right, Jase, up you go." The ladder that rose up the tree seemed to be endless. It was still dark, so I couldn't see the top, which was probably a good thing. My dad seemed to sense my anxiety about climbing the ladder, so he told me, "Don't look down." I started up the tree and quickly realized I would have to get on my tiptoes to reach every board. My dad was right on my heels and offered me encouragement along the way.

When I arrived at my destination, I was bewildered that men could build such a tree house. The duck blind was built into the middle of the tree, probably thirty feet off the ground. After a quick but very stern lesson in shotgun safety from my dad, the sounds of night began morphing into the quietness of dawn. The sun was starting to rise, revealing the open water of Moss Lake. My dad had discovered the tree with his brothers Tommy and Jimmy Frank, so it was one of his favorite hunting spots. My dad loaded my gun, and then I listened as he and his buddies quietly talked about the weather and ducks. After my nerves finally calmed, I was startled again when my dad and Mr. Al cranked down on their duck calls. All of a sudden, I heard my dad say, "Cut 'em!" Boom! Boom! Boom! Once I heard their guns fire and saw feathers flying in the sky, I raised the big Magnum 12 and pulled the trigger. The next thing I knew, I was staring up at a soft orange sky. I quickly realized I was lying on my back!

"What are you doing down there?" my dad asked me.

He took the shotgun from my hands.

"You have to lean into it when you shoot, boy!" he said.

"Did I get 'em?" I asked.

I didn't want to tell my dad that I couldn't see over the shooting porch, much less that the shotgun he gave me was taller and heavier than me. I scraped up a few boards and made a step so I could see over the porch. A few minutes later, I heard my dad say, "Shoot him, Jase!" I looked down and saw a pintail drake backpedaling over a raft team of motionless ducks on the water. My dad had failed to inform me about the concept of decoys!

FIRST HUNT

The question that immediately came to my mind was *Why are all those ducks just sitting there?* I started blasting my shotgun.

"Whoa, whoa!" my dad yelled. "Don't shoot the decoys, boy!"

Fortunately, somebody else had nicked the duck I was supposed to shoot, so it was still sitting there. As my dad and his buddies were reloading their guns, I started shooting again and finally connected. Technically, I had struck for the first time, although my shooting efficiency was a bit ragged. Over the next couple of hours, my dad and his buddies offered their advice on how to be a good shot, which actually sounded more like individual campaign speeches on who was the best marksman. Of course, I didn't have the courage to tell them the reason I'd missed so badly was because I actually believed the painted pieces of plastic were live ducks! I only cared that my first hunt was the most fun I'd ever had in my life, even though my ears were ringing and I had excruciating pain in my right shoulder.

Somewhere during my first duck hunt, I found adventure and saw pure excitement in my dad. As we ventured back to our house that day, I was growing more and more eager to explore the outdoors. I felt a sense of peace after the struggles and heartache that led us to the riverbank. Hunting and fishing would become woven into me from that day forward, but it wasn't so much about the sport as whom I was sharing the pursuit with. Hunting and fishing would become passions for me, but more important,

> I didn't want to tell my dad that I couldn't see over the shooting porch, much less that the shotgun he gave me was taller and heavier than me.

they were something I wanted to share with my dad, brothers, and friends. I also learned another valuable lesson that day, one that I would share with many other people over the years. For some reason, many hunters believe shooting a duck on the water is unsportsmanlike conduct. I've never viewed hunting as a sport, but more of a chase that provides us with a food source. I also believe hunting is God's plan for humans to manage the animal kingdom. The only two things I know ducks are good for are viewing and eating. It doesn't bother me if people don't choose to eat them. I've always said people are free to watch them, eat them, or watch me eat them! This is a fact: ducks taste the same regardless of whether you shoot them when they're flying or sitting! The difficult challenge in duck hunting is tricking a wild duck into flying or swimming into shooting range, because humans aren't the only predators pursuing them. The pursuit is what I love the most about hunting. The actual shooting is the easy part, especially if you get them close enough. The choice of whether to shoot ducks that are sitting, swimming, or flying is a choice that is earned, and I enjoy the decision whatever it may be. Hunting also revealed to me the differences between humans and animals. We use weapons to kill our prey and then season them when we cook and eat them. Even though animals hunt one another, they function only by instinct and are void of seasoning and recipes. I'm not a big fan of zoos because they tend to manipulate animals' natural instincts. I'd rather see them running free in their natural environments. I don't necessarily think having a zoo is wrong or inhumane, because humans are in charge, but I don't like to stare at caged animals and surely don't like to pay an entrance fee to do it! I'll go to the woods for free. Some people might be surprised by this admission, but I've never mounted a fish or animal to hang on my wall. I've never mounted any animal as a trophy. I don't believe it's wrong at all, and plenty of my friends do it, but I don't like having a dead animal staring at me when it looks like it's still alive! I enjoy the pursuit of a hunt. My family has pets and I like animals, but once a year I enjoy proving that humans are at the top of the food chain. Fortunately, there are many such opportunities in Louisiana and our seasoning is extra spicy!

I found the same excitement in hunting frogs and deer for the first time. The first time I went frog-hunting, I was dumbfounded that someone could have that much fun without doing something immoral or illegal. I was the ice chest man on my first hunt, which basically meant every time my dad caught a frog I would quickly open the lid and then shut it before the frog jumped out. I realized the best part was being the catcher. I don't want to brag, but I became one of the greatest frog catchers on the planet. The training was pretty simple—keep the light in their eyes, and when they jump, you jump. The more frogs I ate, the more I sacrificed equipment and my body to obtain as many as the law allowed. I don't classify frogs as "the other white meat"; they're "the only white meat," and then there's everything else.

> I don't classify frogs as "the other white meat"; they're "the only white meat."

I remember the first big buck deer I shot. Phil and I were heading home from a morning duck hunt with a couple of buddies. We were navigating a small creek in our fishing boat, and my dad told me to be on the lookout for deer. We came around a bend in the creek, and my dad shut the motor off and chaotically admonished me to get my gun. He tossed me a buckshot shell, and as I was loading my gun, I looked up on the bank and there was a deer just standing there. Phil was trying to whisper as he said, "Shoot him, Jase! You better hurry." I raised my gun and took the shot. The deer ran toward us in the creek. He went under the water out of sight, and I was waving the gun around exclaiming, "Give me another shell." In a calm voice, my dad said, "Hey, Jase, deer are not like beavers. He is not coming up for air. You got him, son." I started stripping off my clothes to go after the deer. But then my dad informed me the water was thirteen feet deep in the channel of the creek, so the deer wasn't going anywhere.

We went home and made a thirteen-foot-long pole with a giant catfish hook on the end of it. We marched back up the creek and in less than five minutes hooked the deer and brought it into the boat with us. He was a magnificent eight-point buck. We ate the backstraps later that day and processed the rest of the deer. We delivered the rest of the meat to a couple of elderly widows we helped take care of from our church. I kept the deer's horns for a while, but I concluded that I didn't need something to commemorate my first deer hunt. I couldn't forget it if I tried.

As I reflect on the experiences of my first hunts, I'm struck by the fact that they coincided with our new church membership. Maybe some of the godly seeds were being planted in me, but I knew for sure that the backdrop of hunting and fishing was providing me with evidence of a God-created planet. Although the Bible became a blueprint for my life, I didn't realize God existed by reading the pages of a book or listening to a preacher in a church building. Sitting in a church building doesn't make you a Christian, just like sitting in a duck blind doesn't make you a duck hunter. My first thoughts of God came in the outdoors. The more I explored the woods, swamps, and wildlife that lived around our house, the more I concluded that the design of the great outdoors and the rest of our world demanded a Designer. Later in life, I stumbled across Romans 1:20 in the Bible: "For since the creation of the world God's invisible qualities—his eternal power and divine nature—have been clearly seen, being understood from what has been made, so that men are without excuse."

In all my years in the wild, I've never met Mother Nature or Mr. Photosynthesis. Humans tend to try to make sense of things and are always searching for scientific reasons to explain the world's riddles. But if you do not believe in a Creator, your options are limited in trying to explain the functions of Earth, let alone the universe. Who built this place? Where did I come from? Where did you come from? As Hebrews 3:4 says, "For every house is built by someone, but God is the builder of everything." The Hebrews writer was actually comparing Moses and Jesus, but he delivered principles that I have come to believe are fundamental to life's questions. To me it would be silly to claim someone's physical home might not have been built just because you didn't see it being built. We know someone built our homes, neighborhoods, and skyscrapers because of their design, even though they may have been constructed before we were even born.

Hebrews 3:3 tells us: "Jesus has been found worthy of greater honor than Moses, just as the builder of a house has greater honor than the house itself." And Hebrews 3:6 explains: "But Christ is faithful as a son over God's house. And we are his house, if we hold on to our courage and the hope of which we boast." It wasn't until I was fourteen that I put these pieces together, but even before then I saw evidence of God in the outdoors, as well as the transformation of my parents and the people they were associating with. My parents were now living as God's house, and not just on Sunday mornings.

When I was fourteen, I surrendered in baptism and Christ moved in. In John 14:23 Jesus says: "If anyone loves me, he will obey my teaching. My Father will love him, and we will come to him and make our home with him." The good news I heard was that Jesus Christ, God's son, came to this earth as God in flesh; lived a flawless life representing God as perfect, holy, loving, and good; and then died on a cross for the sins of the world. He was buried, only to triumph over death by being bodily resurrected. He stayed forty days, offering much convincing proof that he was alive, only to leave the earth and ascend to the right hand of God, where He functions as mediator for those who trust Him as he awaits His return to take "His house" to the Father, that is, the Creator and Designer. Christ represents us as our advocate in heaven—despite our flaws—and we represent Him on earth. Our relationship with God is based on the One we belong to and the life we live as a result of belonging to our Creator. Our past is forgiven and remembered no more. God uses flawed sons and daughters to make the all-perfect Christ known, and if He can use me, He can use anyone.

> **God uses flawed sons and daughters to make the all-perfect Christ known, and if He can use me, He can use anyone.**

Every time I walk through a swamp or the woods, or climb into a boat on the Ouachita River, I see evidence of God all around me. As far as I'm concerned, that's all the proof I need to know I'm living in His house.

4

······················

BROTHERS IN ARMS

FIGHTING WITH THE BOYS

A friend loves at all times, and a brother
is born for adversity.

—PROVERBS 17:17

I think one of the reasons my family survived its difficult times and is so close today is because we are always laughing at one another's faults and mistakes, and despite whatever injustices are done, we have a good time doing it. We aren't afraid to poke fun at one another and no one ever takes it personal for long. My brothers and I are highly competitive and world-class trash-talkers, and if you ever walk in while we are playing cards or dominoes—just like our games with Granny and Pa—you probably would think someone is fixing to die.

Our neighbor, who was about my parents' age, came over to our house once looking for my mom. She found my brothers and me playing the card game hearts. She offered to be the fourth.

But about midway through the second hand, we looked up and she had tears streaming down her face. She threw her cards in the middle of the table, declared she didn't want to play anymore, and left the house. We were a bit miffed about it and didn't realize until later that our trash talking had led to her emotional exit. Another time, I brought a girl from high school down to my parents' house for supper and cards because she told me she was quite the spades player. Halfway through the game, she was crying hysterically. Her sister later stood nose to nose with me and gave me quite the tongue-lashing. I came to realize that our banter was a bit extreme to people outside of our family. Maybe that is one of the reasons I married a woman who couldn't care less about winning or losing any game.

Our location on the riverbank and our lack of money limited our participation in school sports programs. We followed every season of basketball, baseball, and football with daily epic battles in our yard. The goal of our daily sports games was to win and, more important, dish out the most punishing physical pain possible. In football, the key strategy to keeping your head attached to your body was running out of bounds. We didn't play with pads, so if you came across the middle, you were going down hard to the ground. We weren't worried about getting in trouble when we crushed one another because my dad viewed it as part of the game. He played football at Louisiana Tech and was invited to try out for the Washington Redskins. He was assured that he could beat out the rookie they had drafted—Joe Theismann—but Phil declined. However, Phil believed football was a game that turned boys into men, so he encouraged our backyard antics. It always seemed kind of weird that if I slapped my brother in our room, I would be whipped, but if someone snapped both bones in my arm because I went across the middle in a football game, hey, it was no problem.

Yes, my arm was severely broken one time. In baseball we used the hardest ball we could find, and you made an out by pegging the runner with it. The winner of games was often decided not by runs but by the last man left standing! In basketball, the punishment came from saving the ball from going out of bounds. If you could bounce the ball off your brother's face before it went out of bounds, you would maintain possession. Whether you drew blood or not, it was a legal play. Nowhere in the rules of basketball does it put a limit on how hard you can throw the ball at your opponent, nor does it dictate which body part should do the reflecting. Let's just say every time anyone got near the out-of-bounds lines, everyone else got nervous. I had my nose broken twice on such plays, and one of our buddies actually lost a tooth. It was rough, but, hey, it was part of the game and a great way to vent pent-up frustrations. Even though my brothers and I had our fair share of physical fights growing up, like most teenage brothers do, we always had one another's backs in the end. Even though we had our angry moments, my brothers were still my best friends. We hunted, fished, and played sports together, just like we do today, just with a little less violence.

> If you could bounce the ball off your brother's face before it went out of bounds, you would maintain possession.

I don't think there's any question our competitive personalities come from our parents. My parents liked to fuss and argue, but they rarely raised their voices at each other, at least not in a malicious way. If you lived in the Robertson house, you had to be prepared to defend yourself if you made a mistake. Everyone was going to critique and criticize your poor decisions, whether you were cooking, hunting, fishing, or working.

Both of my parents are excellent cooks, and I think food was the difference maker for us when it came to making friends. Although we didn't have much money and might have looked poor in terms of our clothes, once kids came to our house, most of them never said anything mean about us again because they wanted to be invited back to eat. But some of my friends were probably surprised by what they witnessed at our dinner table.

My mom has always been famous for her biscuits, and we ate them almost every day while I was growing up. One night, we gathered around the table for dinner, and my dad was on a rant about weather, ducks, and just about everything else on his mind. My brothers and I were sitting at the table, but we were waiting for my dad to make his plate before we served ourselves. That was one of the rules in my house: the adults always had the first choice of food before the kids, so we were usually left fighting for whatever was left. Well, on this particular night, I'd snuck a biscuit to the table and was taking small bites of it because I was starving. After a couple of bites, I realized something wasn't quite right about it. It was missing an ingredient and didn't taste very good. I knew my dad was in for a surprise when he sat down to eat.

After my dad took a bite of the biscuit, he chewed about three times and spit it out on the floor.

"Well, these aren't right," he said.

I'll never forget what my dad did next. He walked into the kitchen, grabbed the pan of biscuits, and went to the front door. He opened the door and threw the pan into the front yard! We could hear the dogs scurrying and barking over the commotion.

My dad walked back into the dining room and said, "You know they're bad when the dogs won't even eat them! I'll show you how to make some biscuits."

"Phil, that was my good pan!" my mom yelled.

She was obviously concerned that my dad had broken her favorite pan, but then he started going into this long, drawn-out speech about the proper way to make biscuits. For the next thirty minutes, my mom and dad tried to figure out what went wrong with her buttermilk biscuits, as my dad pulled out the flour, eggs, and everything else he needed to make a second batch. It's the way it was in the Robertson house: you had to assess blame and critique what went wrong before you could move on. If something wasn't right, there wasn't an excuse and you certainly weren't getting any sympathy from anyone else. The culprit was getting blamed for it!

> It's the way it was in the Robertson house: you had to assess blame and critique what went wrong before you could move on.

In my teenage years, I had a horrific wreck that totaled the family truck just up the road from our house. I wasn't paying attention and pulled out in front of a very large truck and trailer going about fifty miles per hour. My truck spun, flipped, and crashed into a light pole. I didn't have my seat belt on and was battered, cut, and bruised all over my body, although miraculously none of the injuries turned out to be that severe. I was lying on the ground covered in blood with a piece of glass about six inches long sticking out of my chin when I regained consciousness. When I opened my eyes, my dad was standing over me. His first words were, "What were you thinking?" Thanks, Dad, I was just happy to be alive. Despite my family's propensity to assess blame while withholding compassion, these moments became stories that we laugh at now and retell over and over again.

As I've said before, my dad didn't have many rules. He told us that as long as we passed in school and stayed out of trouble, we could do anything we wanted. He was a man of his word. I think that's one of the reasons I was a fairly good kid and didn't cross him. There were plenty of chances to step out of line. There were a lot of days when I didn't even know where my parents were. But I was living in a controlled environment, either fishing on the river or hunting in the woods, and there was nothing else to do. I had more fun fishing and hunting than doing anything in town, which might have led me to trouble. I never had curfews, and there wasn't a lot of trouble to find in the middle of nowhere. I always viewed darkness as my curfew unless I could find a flashlight. You were at the end of a dirt road and surrounded by water.

What were you going to do other than hunt and fish? I didn't have a vehicle to drive until my later teen years, so it wasn't like I was going anywhere. And there wasn't anyone else to influence me into making bad decisions, other than my brothers.

Like I said before, I didn't drink and didn't do drugs. I made the decision not to drink before I even became a Christian. I remembered the things associated with the honky-tonk bar my dad owned, and I vowed I wasn't going to do anything to put myself in a position where I could wind up in prison or dead. I decided I was going to wait until I was thirty years old before I'd ever have any kind of drink, which is about what I did. My logic was that I would be mature enough to handle it by then.

I rarely drink alcohol now and have concluded that if you're not doing it to get a buzz, it must be more of an acquired taste, because it doesn't taste very good to me. I stay away from drinking more than one or two drinks in a twenty-four-hour period, just in case I find something I like. It's been a good system for me. My buddies tried to tempt me in high school, and I always told them, "Nothing in a bottle or can is going to make me feel better than catching a mess of frogs or shooting ducks." They were always perplexed by my answer, but I never was one to care about peer pressure or what people said about me.

> I vowed I wasn't going to do anything to put myself in a position where I could wind up in prison or dead.

My brother Alan is older than me and suffered more consequences from being raised in the bar. Willie and I were younger, so being around the bar probably didn't affect us as much. Alan struggled with alcohol in high school and even left home for a while. I tried to tell my parents my brother was cutting up on several occasions, but he was pretty good at getting out of trouble. I remember seeing a washtub full of empty beer bottles in the trunk of his car, and I told my mom about it. When she confronted him, he explained to her that he and a couple of buddies were helping a Louisiana litter-free cause and they'd cleaned up a sandbar on the river. She believed him! Alan and his friends whipped my rear over telling my mom, so I kept future discoveries to myself. My parents eventually sent him packing, and he moved to New Orleans.

But after Alan was badly beaten in a fight in New Orleans, he returned home and underwent a complete life change. I remember the day he called home as we were in the middle of a domino game. My dad told him over the phone he was welcome back but had to meet him up the road for a talk. I immediately thought of Luke 15:20: "So he got up and went to his father. But while he was still a long way off, his father saw him and was filled with compassion for him; he ran to his son, threw his arms around him and kissed him."

I'm sure there wasn't a whole lot of hugging and kissing from my dad, but I was proud they hadn't burned the bridge back home, even though we were all a bit bitter and frustrated with Alan's choices. God teaches us to love the sinner while hating the sins they commit, and God welcomes everyone with open arms regardless of what they have done. Like my dad had done, Al surrendered to Christ, and he eventually became a minister. Jep, my youngest brother, wasn't born until after my father became a Christian, so he never witnessed any of my dad's wild days. But Jep also struggled with drugs and alcohol and left the flock in high school, only to return to my family and the Lord after I, my brothers, and Dad had a type of intervention with him. He was overwhelmed with emotion and confessed to us the bad things he had been doing. That was the only time I can recall seeing every one of us with tears in our eyes at the same time. We gathered around him, put our hands on him, and prayed together. James 5:16 states: "Therefore confess your sins to each other and pray for each other so that you may be healed. The prayer of a righteous man is powerful and effective."

My brothers and I were allowed to argue and debate all we wanted, but once meat started popping, my dad stepped in. He didn't care who started the fight or ended it. If there was any kind of physical fracas, everyone involved was getting whipped! In hindsight, it was actually a failed policy. I remember one time I accidentally hit Willie in the nose and it started pouring out blood. We were wrestling and playing around in the yard, and I inadvertently hit him. It really was an accident. Willie started teasing me, telling me he was going to tell Dad I hit him in the nose on purpose. My dad always said, "First blood, you're going to get whipped."

As Willie ran off to tell my dad, it hit me that I'd better get my money's worth if I was going to get whipped, so I chased Willie down and started beating the snot out of him! My dad pulled up and saw us fighting in the front yard. For some reason, I told my dad the complete truth, thinking that would help my chances. Boy, it was the one of the worst whippings I'd ever received, but at least the crime fit the punishment!

There were a couple of times I was whipped when I didn't deserve to be punished, which is another reason my dad's philosophy was flawed. One day, Alan and Willie were fighting near where we dipped the duck calls in tung oil. My dad walked out, heard the commotion, and immediately thought all of us were fighting. He whipped every one of us, but I didn't have anything to do with it! The worst part was as my dad was about to whip me with a belt, I grabbed the board where we hung the duck calls to dry. It had rows of nails sticking out of it! The nails poked through my hands, and I screamed before my dad even whipped me. Of course, my dad made a big deal out of it. "I haven't even hit you, and you're already screaming," he said. Never mind that blood was pouring from my hands. Fortunately, they were only superficial wounds.

Well, I was so mad about getting whipped for nothing that I went into my bedroom, packed a bag, and headed for the woods. Whenever I felt like I'd been wronged, I ran away. At that age, I was still struggling to understand why my dad had left his family during his wild days, so I figured running away was the answer to just about every injustice in my life. I took off down the road and went about a mile before I realized I didn't have any food. I had some weapons with me, but I didn't have a gun, so I couldn't shoot anything to eat. After contemplating my dilemma for a few minutes, I turned around and headed home. I figured I'd probably given them enough punishment for wronging me, and I was certain my mom and dad were sick to their stomachs from their anxiety about my leaving.

> Well, I was so mad about getting whipped for nothing that I went into my bedroom, packed a bag, and headed for the woods.

When I walked into our house, my parents and brothers were sitting around the table eating lunch! I heard them talking, but they weren't worrying about me! It was like I'd never left. They didn't even act like they cared that I'd run away. I thought to myself, *Huh, isn't this something?* So I went back outside and climbed up on the roof of the house. I sat there for a couple of hours and nothing happened. Nobody came looking for me, and they went about their normal business. Then it got to be nightfall and I started smelling fried squirrel, and I didn't hear anybody say anything about going to look for Jase. So I climbed down from the roof and went into the house. No one said anything to me. They didn't even ask me where I'd been! I probably ran away ten times when I was a kid, and not once did anyone come looking for me.

Probably the scariest moment of my childhood occurred when Jep was about three years old. He wandered off from the yard and no one could find him. We always had Labrador retrievers as our hunting dogs, but one in particular didn't like to duck-hunt. His name was Gabe, and no matter how hard my dad tried, he couldn't turn the dog into a retriever. He was black and had a white patch on his neck. My dad said, "He's not full bred and that's why he's worthless." We turned Gabe into a house dog and he ended up becoming my favorite pet. After several frightening minutes of not being able to find Jep, we went to the riverbank and found him. Gabe was standing in front of Jep, almost blocking him from going into the water. If Jep had fallen into the river, he would have drowned. It was almost as if the dog was protecting him. Gabe ended up being a really smart dog and always seemed to be looking out for us. On a couple of occasions, he stopped in front of me on the riverbank and would start to growl. As I looked around I would discover he was growling at a cottonmouth. What I found strange is that he would not growl at non-poisonous snakes; that alone made him smarter than a lot of people I know! Even his death was pretty smart. He was old and had gotten really sick, so he waded neck-deep at the edge of the river and just stood there for two days. We would call him and he wouldn't come. By the third day, I got up from bed and went down to the river to see if he was still there and he was gone.

Al was always the instigator. One night, I was lying on the couch watching TV, and Al and his friends were throwing things at me. They loved to pick on me and pester me because they were older and bigger than me. Of course, my dad was in the room, but he was oblivious to what was going on. He was blowing on duck calls and packaging them to sell. All of a sudden, Al threw a shotgun shell and it hit me on top of the head. It knocked me out cold! When I regained consciousness, my dad was beating the fire out of Al! That was one time Al was busted. He always seemed to get away with everything. He'd start a fight between Willie and me and then we'd get punished for it. But Al was the one who always started trouble.

BROTHERS IN ARMS

Al loved to pick on me when I was sleeping, which was when I was most vulnerable. After a few incidents, I started sleeping with rocks and batteries. When I sensed Al and his friends were coming after me, I came up firing. Holes covered the walls and doors of our bedroom, and they were the product of pure meanness as we threw things at one another. The one instance I felt really bad about was when I was awakened thinking Al was in the room. Since it was dark, I reached to find some sort of weapon. I grabbed the alarm clock and flung it as hard as I could. I heard a loud thud, a cry of pain, and another loud thud as the perpetrator hit the floor. I jumped up, turned on the lights, and realized that I'd knocked Jep out cold. He was just passing through but happened to be in the wrong place at the wrong time. I still don't know where my parents were when all of this was occurring. It was survival of the fittest.

I always whipped Willie because I was older. I had the upper hand on him, but Al always got the best of me. Al was five years older than me, but the last time we sparred, I won through what might not have been fair tactics. I knew Al had knee problems from playing sports in recreational leagues. Shortly after Al graduated from high school, he and his friends came to our house and started messing with me. As they were walking away, I took off after him. Al must have sensed I was coming after him, because he turned around just before I reached him. I lowered my shoulder and took his bad knee out. He fell to the ground in a heap. He was in agony.

"Hey, if you don't quit messing with me, I'm going to do this every time you turn away," I told him.

It was the last time Al and his friends ever messed with me. Willie and I also had our share of physical fights, but he learned to leave me alone, too. We have the same relationship in business now. When my parents decided to turn over the Duck Commander business, I think they assumed I would run it because I knew how to make the duck calls better than anyone else. But I didn't want anything to do with the business part of it. I didn't want the responsibility or stress of dealing with customers, and I certainly didn't want the business interfering with duck season. So when my parents sat me down to talk about it, I told them I didn't want the company. I told them I was perfectly content making the duck calls. So my parents offered Willie the company, and he and his wife, Korie, agreed to take over Duck Commander.

> When my parents decided to turn over the Duck Commander business, I think they assumed I would run it because I knew how to make the duck calls better than anyone else.

Willie and I talked shortly thereafter, and I told him, "Look, I'll do the duck calls. You do the business. You can make all the money if you want to take all the risks, it's fine with me." I liked what I was doing, and it was providing a good life for my family. I didn't want to be consumed by the day-to-day operations of Duck Commander to the point where it would take time away from my wife or kids. I commend Willie for the job he's done with the company. He has taken it to heights none of us could have imagined, and he's worked hard to make it happen. He has a very good business mind and sees the big picture, despite the fact that he annoys the heck out of me sometimes. I often tell people that having your brother as a boss is like dating your cousin—it's a bit weird!

For me, life has never been about the pursuit of fortune and fame. I've never been a materialistic guy and don't need a lot of money. I think it goes back to my childhood, when we had almost nothing in terms of money or material possessions, but I thought my life was perfect. I was happy living on the river, catching fish, hunting, eating well, and playing dominoes.

My relationship with my brothers really hasn't changed much in adulthood. We're still best friends and go hunting and fishing together as much as we can. Of course, we don't physically fight anymore; one of us might end up in the hospital if we did. Willie's my boss, but he learned a long time ago to leave me alone and let me do my job. He knows deep down I take a lot of pride in making the duck calls and ensuring that every one of them sounds perfect. Sure, we have our disagreements from time to time, but he's still my brother and one of my best friends. I mean, we're brothers. What's he going to do, fire me?

5

-----◆-----

HIGH SCHOOL DAYS

BECOMING AN INFLUENCER FOR GOOD

Therefore go and make disciples of all nations,
baptizing them in the name of the Father and of the
Son and of the Holy Spirit.

—MATTHEW 28:19

In 2008, an Australian company commissioned a study to find out exactly how much people fear public speaking. The survey of more than one thousand people found that 23 percent feared public speaking more than death itself! As Jerry Seinfeld once said, most people attending a funeral would rather be in the casket than delivering the eulogy!

I can relate to those people because I feared speaking in front of a class or group of people more than anything else when I was a kid. In fact, I dropped speech in high school because when I signed up for it I thought it was a grammar class for an English credit. When I found out it actually required giving an oral presentation, I didn't want any part of it! After hearing the overview of the class on the first day, I got out of my seat and walked toward the door; the teacher asked me where I was going. We had a brief meeting in the hall, in which she informed me that nobody ever dropped her class. After a meeting with the principal, I dropped the class, but on the condition that I might be called upon in the near future to use my hunting and fishing skills. I thought the principal was joking—until I was called upon later that year during duck season to pick ducks during recess! I looked at it as a fair trade.

I believe the circumstances of my childhood set up a perfect path for me to be used by God. At fourteen, I came to understand God's message, and my baptism in the Ouachita River provided me with a peace about my relationship with Him. But my biggest hurdle in becoming one of God's disciples was my shy disposition. My personality has always been laid-back, and as I mentioned before, I think my dad's wild days in my childhood contributed to my becoming introverted. As I became a teenager, I still didn't say much, and my Christian life was really about trying to avoid doing things that were wrong. As some of my friends began to experiment with sex, drugs, and alcohol, I simply tried to survive as a Christian.

I remember a summer night after my baptism when a campout with my buddies became very uncomfortable. We had camped out before, but on this night two of the guys brought a couple of beers, a huge marijuana joint, and some nude magazines. I was trying to figure out how I was going to get out of the situation when suddenly we heard people chattering in the woods. It turned out to be my buddy's youth group from his church on a bit of a surprise visit. There was a mad scramble, and all the evidence was hidden. It felt weird listening to everyone sing around the campfire, thinking of what might have happened. After they left our campsite, I did take a stand and said I wouldn't be participating in any of the extracurricular activities that were planned. Fortunately, everyone agreed not to as well. However, that became my last campout with those guys, as I was never invited back again.

Since I decided at an early age that I would avoid the former life of my dad, if for no other reason than the fear of what that life produced, I didn't experience peer pressure while I was growing up. Sure, I had opportunities to get into trouble with the temptations of alcohol, drugs, and sex, but I decided that those weren't things I was going to experiment with. My safe havens were hunting in the woods and fishing the river near our house. Because I became such an accomplished fisherman and hunter, I gained the little popularity I needed. I would share my daily hunting and fishing adventures with my buddies at school, but once the conversation turned to immorality I would slip away and move on.

> Two of the guys brought a couple of beers, a huge marijuana joint, and some nude magazines.

My parents have always been vocal about "the birds and the bees." People who watched the *Duck Dynasty* episode in which my dad gave Willie's son John Luke and his girlfriend the sex talk while motoring down the river in a boat might not be surprised that I heard this exact speech countless times in my childhood. I remember coming home one day after hearing my buddies talking about sexually transmitted diseases and asking my dad about it. I don't remember the specifics of his speech, but I would never forget the last thing he said. "Son, you keep that thing in your pocket until you get married and you'll never have to worry about it," he told me. The timing of our conversation was perfect when it came to my staying sexually pure.

The previous year, I had really taken an interest in the opposite sex, but it all seemed pretty natural. It all changed one night when I was in the ninth grade. I went with a buddy to a swimming party, where we met two girls whom we were both interested in. As the night wore on, we found ourselves alone in a room with the girls. The girl I liked asked me to help her undress. I was very attracted to her, and she was pretty healthy for a ninth grader. As I looked back at my buddy cheering me on, the only thing I could think of was my dad's admonition—and three letters, R-U-N! I ran out of the room, and the abuse I took from my buddies over the next few days was probably the worst I ever experienced. From then on, I decided to shy away from girls with questionable reputations and focus on those who could possibly help me spiritually and help get me to heaven. I didn't feel I was strong enough to stay pure unless both parties had the same goal.

"Son, you keep that thing in your pocket until you get married and you'll never have to worry about STDs."

I eventually came up with a plan of action. On the first date, I would share my faith with the girl and declare my intention to wait until marriage before having sex. In a way this held me accountable, and it also got rid of any girls who had a quick roll in the hay in mind. I also decided to stay away from "the second look"—noticing a good-looking woman, then dwelling on her for a second, more lustful look. I tried to notice the beauty and feel the attraction to a woman but ultimately pursue her spiritual makeup. It wasn't always easy and I oftentimes fell short, but I kept trying. God changes us from the inside out, and that helps us look at other people the same way. But it's hard to break the habit of that second look. So I would think about hunting situations to help me in my struggle. I remember thinking that when it came to dating there was a thin line between becoming a trophy buck hanging out in a woman's living room for life and being just another dead deer carcass in a ditch run over by a woman driver. Trophy bucks do not come easily, and my pride, which some girls viewed as arrogance, actually helped me stay pure.

The surprise for me was that my lack of interest in having premarital sex seemed to only fuel girls' interest in me. I think playing "hard to get" was a sign of strength, and it made me different from most guys. I have to be honest: I did experience a certain thrill from being chased by the other sex. But in the end, my relationships with girls usually ended after the Gospel speech or when I informed them that hunting and fishing were a lot more fun (and important) than having a relationship based on pure physical attraction. My plan was to stick to hunting ducks and frogs and not women.

As I reached the age of sixteen, I was really battling with being vocal about my faith. My friends seemed so vile, and I knew they probably weren't mature enough to seriously consider what I wanted to tell them. I wanted to share what I was doing and what I believed with my friends, but I didn't have the courage to do it. I believed that if my friends knew what I knew, they wouldn't be doing what they were doing. I was studying the Bible and read Philemon 1:6: "I pray that you may be active in sharing your faith, so that you will have a full understanding of every good thing we have in Christ."

At some point in high school, I finally realized that being indwelled by the Holy Spirit and having God with me were not things I needed to be shy about. As I matured and became more confident, and as my family's spiritual growth continued, I started to spread God's message more and more. Somewhere in this process, I stumbled upon the greatest way to keep myself free from drugs, alcohol abuse, and premarital sex, and it wasn't about just saying no. Second Corinthians 1:18–20 says that our message is not about saying yes and no, but in Christ it is always *yes*. The more often you give someone the reasons to say yes to Christ, the less you find yourself having to say no. By becoming the aggressor in sharing the good news of Christ with everyone in earshot, I became the one doing the influencing for good rather than the one being influenced for evil. I deduced that my Christianity is not about me but about Christ living through me. Jesus Christ represents everything that is truly good about me.

Oddly enough, it started with a prank telephone call when I was seventeen.

As I was studying the Bible one night, I had just said a prayer in which I asked God for the strength to be more vocal about my faith. All of a sudden, the phone rang and I answered.

"Hello?" I asked.

No one answered.

"Hello?" I asked again.

There was still silence on the other end. I started to hang up the phone, but then it hit me.

"I'm glad you called," I said. "You're just the person I'm looking for."

Much to my surprise, the person on the other end didn't hang up.

> "I want to share something with you that I'm really excited about, and you're the perfect person to hear it."

"I want to share something with you that I'm really excited about," I said. "It's what I put my faith in. You're the perfect person to hear it."

So then I started sharing the Gospel, and whoever was on the other end never said a word. Every few minutes, I'd hear a little sound, so I knew the person was still listening. After several minutes, I told the person, "I'm going to ask you a few questions. Why don't you do one beep for no and two beeps for yes? We can play that game." The person on the other end didn't say anything.

Undaunted by the person's silence, I took out my Bible and started reading scripture. After a few minutes, I heard pages rustling on the other end of the phone. I knew the person was reading along with me! After a while, every noise I heard got me more excited! At one point, I heard a baby crying in the background. I guessed that the person on the phone was a mother or perhaps a babysitter. I asked her if she needed to go care for her child. She set the phone down and came back a few minutes later. I figured that once I started preaching, she would hang up the phone. But the fact that she didn't got my adrenaline flowing. For three consecutive hours, I shared the message of God I'd heard from my little church in Luna, Louisiana, and what I'd learned by studying the Bible and listening to others talk about their faith over the last two years. By the time our telephone call ended, I was out of material!

"Hey, will you call back tomorrow night?" I asked her.

She didn't say anything and hung up the phone. I wasn't sure she would call me back the next night. But I hoped she would, and I prepared for what I was going to share with her next. I came across a medical account of Jesus' death and decided to use it. It was a very graphic account of Jesus dying on a cross.

Around ten o'clock the next night, the phone rang. I answered it and there was silence on the other end. My blood and adrenaline started pumping once again! Our second conversation didn't last as long because I came out firing bullets! I worried my account of Jesus' death was too graphic and might offend her. But as I told her the story of Jesus' crucifixion—how He was sentenced to death by Pontius Pilate, beaten with leather-thonged whips, required to strip naked, forced to wear a crown of thorns on His head, and then crucified with nails staked through His wrists and ankles—I started to hear sobs on the other end of the phone.

Then I heard her cry and she hung up the phone. She never called back.

Although I never talked to the woman again or learned her identity, my conversations with her empowered me to share the Lord's message with my friends and even strangers. I came to truly realize it was not about me but about the power in the message of Christ. When I attended a football game at West Monroe High School with a few buddies the next fall, a few of them started giving me grief about my faith in Christ. After a few good minutes of ribbing, I looked at Blake Gaston, my best friend, and asked him three questions.

"How did you get on earth? What are you supposed to be doing here? How are you leaving?" I asked him.

None of my friends could offer me good answers at the time. One of them said he came from his momma, and a few others cracked crude jokes. Blake informed me he had a date with a flaming-hot redhead later that night, and there was no way he was going to miss out on possibly getting physical with her. We went our separate ways. They believed I was a Bible-thumping radical, and I wasn't interested in participating in what they were doing. I went home that night and made a list of about a hundred friends I wanted to share the Gospel with.

Over the next two years, I went back to every one of my friends who'd ridiculed me at the football game, sat down with each of them face-to-face, and told them about my faith. My family and I ended up baptizing most of them in the river by our house. A lot of those guys are still my best friends and attend our church today. The first one I actually brought to the Lord was Blake. He called me a couple years after our confrontation and asked if he could come fishing with me. I had never burned the bridge of our relationship, and eventually I had asked him to be a groomsman in my wedding. I knew his heart was troubled and the redhead he had been so enamored with was long gone. He spent the next few days with me at my house, and we talked about his past, and he listened intently to the good news of Christ. He claimed Christ as Lord, took the same walk to the Ouachita River I had, and was baptized into Christ.

Because of my strong faith, I didn't have a lot of good friends in school. In fact, I only had one very close friend who was also outspoken about her faith. Her name was Angel Gist, and I met her in the ninth grade. She was very vocal about her faith, and that's one of the things that really drew me to her. We were never more than close friends. When I first started dating Missy, we broke up for a short time because another guy asked her out. I didn't know why Missy was talking to him in the first place, so we got into an argument and broke up. I went to Angel's house and sat in her driveway. I wondered if Angel was the woman I needed to be with romantically because of her spirituality. I prayed about it and decided we only needed to be friends.

But Angel and I were best friends for a couple of years. She had a great personality and an incredible sense of humor. We had a lot of fun together, and even though she was very moral, most people viewed her as hysterically funny and cool to be around. She was fearless regarding what anyone thought about her, and her conversations conveyed that. She had so much self-confidence. We studied the Bible together and played basketball at her house. She was the only girl who ever could whip me in basketball.

After high school, Angel received a basketball scholarship to attend Baylor University in Waco, Texas. She started as a freshman and had a really bright future. We had somewhat drifted apart because of the paths of our lives. On February 11, 1989, Angel and one of her classmates at Baylor were killed in a car wreck outside of Dawson, Texas. Their car crossed into the eastbound lane of the highway and struck a pickup truck head-on. Angel and her friend died at the scene. Angel was nineteen.

On the day Angel died, I was with my brothers in Baton Rouge, Louisiana, watching LSU play the University of Tennessee in a basketball game. Somebody called one of my brothers and told him about the accident. My brothers didn't tell me Angel died until we returned to West Monroe a few days later. We were about a mile from my house when my older brother, Al, told me what had happened. I was overcome with emotion and wept bitterly and uncontrollably. It was the only time in my life that I stayed angry with my brothers for an extended period of time. I went to Angel's funeral but couldn't stomach going inside. I later found out her parents wanted me to serve as a pallbearer. I think it might have helped me because I don't think I ever grieved for her properly.

It was a really difficult time in my life because Angel was the most spiritual person I knew on earth. She was like a sister to me, and I visited her burial plot many times alone, trying to cope with her being gone. I couldn't make sense of her death, and it took me a few years to get past it. She was such an influential person in my life, and I realized after she was gone how much I loved her. The only positive I took from her death was that the resurrection became more of a reality for me. Angel provided me with a living example of being vocal about one's faith. I knew I wanted to see her again. I read Hebrews 12:1, which tell us, "Therefore, since we are surrounded by such a great cloud of witnesses, let us throw off everything that hinders and the sin that so easily entangles, and let us run with perseverance the race marked out for us. Let us fix our eyes on Jesus, the author and perfecter of our faith." I added Angel to my list of witnesses, and I know I'll see her again.

During my senior year of high school, Tommy Powell, one of my dad's closest friends, asked me to speak to a group of students at a small Christian school in West Monroe. Tommy hunted with us a lot, and he kind of took me under his wing and offered me advice about a lot of life's lessons. The thing I really liked about Tommy was that he was always so positive. Every time Tommy went hunting with us, he was the most optimistic hunter I have ever shared a blind with. I guess Tommy saw potential in me from a spiritual standpoint. More than anything else, I think he realized I was serious about my faith. Tommy isn't a dynamic guy by any stretch of the imagination, but I think in the Lord you try to find ways to help people out. I think mentoring me was his opportunity to help someone.

When Tommy asked me to speak to the students, I immediately told him no. I was finally comfortable talking to people individually about my faith, but I still didn't want anything to do with public speaking. But then I thought about the idea for three or four days and it was really nagging at me. I called Tommy back and told him to line it up.

When I arrived at the classroom a few days later, there were about fifty kids there. I stood in the front of the class and told them I was a hunter and fisherman, but I loved the Lord, and I told them why. I went through my entire testimony and shared the Gospel with them. I was so nervous talking to them that every time I tried to turn a page in my Bible, I ripped about three pages! My hand was shaking so badly that I couldn't stop ripping pages! I kept looking up to see if anyone had noticed how nervous I was. I couldn't wait for my talk to end.

But after I was finished talking, a young boy came up to me. He had tears in his eyes.

"Thanks, mister," he said. "I really needed to hear that."

I couldn't believe God had used a simple guy like me to have this kind of impact on a kid. The youth director at White's Ferry Road Church heard about my speech and asked me to talk to a group of students at Ouachita Christian School a couple of

> I was so nervous talking to them that every time I tried to turn a page in my Bible, I ripped about three pages!

weeks later. I begrudgingly agreed, and it was a much bigger audience, but I got through it. The more often I spoke, the more comfortable I was talking in front of people.

The next summer, our youth group took a trip to Florida for a Christian conference. There were three speakers slated for the event, and I was one of them. The first guy who was supposed to talk stood up in a big classroom full of about two hundred kids. He apologized to the audience and said because of his selfishness, he wasn't properly prepared to address them. He sat back down. Now, I was nervous because I was next and he'd just killed the mood in the room. I was about to die! Thankfully, the guy stood back up and gave an excellent talk about standing before God and not being prepared.

Thanks to my parents and people like Angel and Tommy, I know God is using me to help others be prepared to stand before Him, and by doing so I am prepared as well. 1 John 4:17 says: "In this way, love is made complete among us so that we will have confidence on the day of judgment, because in this world we are like him."

ARRANGED DATE

FALLING IN LOVE WITH MISSY

Husbands, love your wives, just as Christ loved the
church and gave himself up for her.

—EPHESIANS 5:25

My dad's favorite motivational slogan when we were kids was "Who's a man?" He used this admonition mostly when there was a tough job to do that required a great deal of physical exertion and pain, like when my brothers and I carried washtubs full of fish up the muddy riverbank. We would often fall, and he would laugh and keep quoting the same motivational line over and over: "Who's a man?" Dad's encouragement—at various decibel levels—always seemed to work.

I felt a sense of pride when my actions answered his challenge, and our work on the river often turned into "strongest man" competitions between my brothers and me. My dad has always viewed manhood as a big deal; he likes to say the most endangered species on the planet is manly men. As I began to become interested in girls, he would encourage me to work even harder, because what kind of woman doesn't like a man with muscles? After one brutal day of hard work on the river, he told me, "One day you'll be able to grow whiskers on your chin to go along with these muscles I'm giving you. These girls will recognize you as a man from a distance."

Of course, there was a bit of a power struggle between my mom and dad over how my brothers and I looked as we became older. My mom would spend my dad's hard-earned money on a few nice clothes for us when we started dating, and my dad would roll his eyes and shake his head. There is something to be said for first impressions, and my mom knew that if I was going to get a nice girl, something had to be done about my ragged appearance (not to mention my scent of sweat and fish). My dad, on the other hand, focused his efforts on dating advice. One of his favorite quotes was: "A situation becomes a crisis when cattle or women stampede." I decided to try to find a balance between by parents' ideas on dating. One of the things I really liked about White's Ferry Road Church was that it was a big church with an active youth group. When we attended the smaller country church, I felt alone because there weren't many kids my age in the congregation. I didn't have many spiritual friends, other than Angel, and she attended a different church and high school. At White's Ferry Road Church, my brother Willie and I found the greatest pool of potential girlfriends who were spiritual that any boy could have wanted. Willie and I started dating every one of the girls, simultaneously if possible! We even dated the same girl sometimes! It was a different date every other night.

I applied a lot of what I knew about fishing to the dating world. I thought that women were a lot like fish in that they travel around in packs. They even go to the bathroom together—even if some of them don't need to go! The key to catching a lot of fish is to get the pack caught up in the frenzy of trying to be the one to capture the lure. When fish feed, they are motivated by one another. I have watched fish go crazy when my lure splashes across the top of the water. I have even caught two fish on one lure several times in large schools of feeding fish. However, I eventually learned the hard way that women are not like fish at all. For one, fish do not have the ability to slap your face because you're trying to land two at once. Second, fishing is relaxing and relieves stress, while dating a lot of girls at the same time is maddening. Luckily for me, I always had the woods and water to escape to when things got crazy, which seemed to happen a lot. Nothing tells a girl that you've moved on quite like a dead deer in the back of your truck or ducks on the grill.

> I eventually learned the hard way that women are not like fish at all. For one, fish do not have the ability to slap your face because you're trying to land two at once.

After a while, I started talking to one particular girl and we started hanging out, or at least that's what we called it at the time. I might have kissed her two or three times, but it really wasn't much of a relationship romantically. She initially came to me for spiritual advice, and I offered to help her. She was very attractive and seemed really nice. I was at her house one

Sunday after church, and she came downstairs and told me I needed to leave. I didn't know what the deal was, but I left and walked outside. All of a sudden, this guy came tearing into her driveway in a pickup truck. I'd never seen the guy before in my life, but he jumped out of his truck and charged at me. He started screaming at me, calling me every bad word in the book. I looked behind me to make sure he was talking to me, but there was nobody else there. I thought he had me confused with someone else.

But then I realized the guy was the reason the girl wanted me to leave. He was her boyfriend and wasn't happy! When I figured out what was going on, I was like, "Well, come on over here, son. I'll kick your tail! I don't even know who you are." Thankfully, he calmed down and backed off.

"Let's just talk," he told me.

"All right," I said. "Let's take a ride."

When I got into the guy's truck, he started screaming and threatening me again! He told me about how he was fixing to mangle my body, and it really kind of scared me a little bit. During our conversation, he explained to me that he was doing more than hanging out with the girl I'd just left. They had a long-term relationship and were a lot more involved than I realized.

"Hey, you can have her," I told him. "I was only checking her out. She never told me she had a boyfriend."

I told the guy I wasn't interested in the girl and didn't want to fight him.

"Let me tell you what I'm really in on," I said.

Then I started telling him about the Gospel, but the more I shared God's Word with him, the madder he became! Eventually, he pulled off at a dead-end road. When he stopped, I figured out that he wasn't getting the gist of my message! Since I'd shared the Gospel with him and I'd already told him I wasn't going to fight him, I decided I was going to turn the other cheek and swallow my pride.

"I only have one thing to ask," I told him. "Don't hit me in the face."

The guy punched me about three or four times, but luckily my adrenaline was really pumping, so it didn't seem to hurt much, and he stayed away from my face. The guy climbed back in his truck, and for a few seconds I feared he was going to run me over. He left me in the middle of nowhere, about three miles from town. After I walked a couple of miles, the girl's parents, of all people, saw me walking down the road and picked me up. I didn't tell them anything. I asked them to take me to Johnny and Chrys Howard's house, so I could attend teen church. Johnny and Chrys are Willie's in-laws; we had teen church at his future wife Korie's house nearly every Sunday when we were in high school.

When I arrived at Korie's house, I was a little bit bruised up, but my pride hurt a lot more. I could hear my dad's admonitions of "Who's a man?" echoing in my mind. Even though I felt like I did a godly thing, it was very humiliating and humbling. The girl who kicked me out of her house was there, and she tried to apologize to me.

"Hey, I'm done with you," I told her. "You're out."

GOOD CALL

The ironic part of the story is that Missy was pretty good friends with the girl who kicked me out of her house. On the night of the incident, details of my fight spread like wildfire through our youth group. Missy pulled me outside and talked to me about it. For some odd reason, I came up with a brilliant idea.

"Why don't we go to the football game this Friday night as a couple?" I told Missy. "It will really make her jealous."

Missy wasn't too happy with the girl, so she happily agreed to do it. Five days later, Missy and I went out on our fake date. I picked her up and we headed to one of her school's football games. Our primary goal that night was just to be seen together by the girl. However, we actually had a great time together, and I thought I sensed a mutual attraction. To be honest, what really piqued my interest in her was that when I took her home that night, she got out of my truck and walked inside. She didn't say much and didn't expect a good-night chat. I figured our orchestrated relationship was over. To me, the date was a good way to show everyone I had moved on by watching the game with a good-looking woman on my arm.

The next Sunday, I was at church and somebody tapped me on the shoulder.

"Look who's here," my buddy told me.

It was the guy who had beat me up and left me at the dead-end road! I thought he was following me around, because he was looking at me. It aroused my anger, and I was prepared to fight him in the parking lot after church was over! Whether I got whipped or not, I was going to let him know that I wasn't going to put up with his stalking me. When he walked up to me in the parking lot after church, I was so close to hitting him between the eyes. But when I looked at him, I could tell he was broken.

"Whatcha got?" I asked him.

> **I was prepared to fight him in the parking lot after church was over!**

"I know this is going to sound weird," he said. "But you know when you were talking to me about the resurrection? I'd never heard that before. Forget the girl. This ain't about the girl. I want to study the Bible and learn about what you told me."

It crossed my mind that he might have some devious ploy to attack my faith, so I decided to seek out someone for advice and wisdom. I found Mike Kellett, the youth director at our church, and we studied the Bible with him. The guy was converted, and we baptized him in the Howards' swimming pool. He began meeting at our church and later became a pilot. Over the years, he has flown me free of charge to a couple of speaking engagements where I delivered the same Gospel message that I shared with him. We worked together as brothers in Christ and became good friends.

His conversion taught me a lot about spiritual warfare. Up until this point, I had judged the strength of a man solely on his toughness and fighting skills. I had been in many physical fights with my brothers and guys from school. I often remind Willie that the reason he is so business savvy is the constant butt-whippings I delivered to him. They molded his decision-making process. But the situation with the guy at church was different, because the threats came from someone I didn't know, and he only insisted on fighting me after I shared the Gospel with him. It was a freak circumstance God used for a greater good, and it really inspired me. Second Corinthians 10:4 tells us, "The weapons we fight with are not the weapons of the world. On the contrary, they have divine power to demolish strongholds." By sharing the good news of Christ, I actually won the fight and I never threw a punch. The message of Christ's death and resurrection transcends the physical makeup of a person and always triggers a spiritual response of anger, sadness, or happiness. It is the ultimate unleashing of power, God's power.

Obviously, I didn't pursue that girl any longer, and I didn't think about Missy much after our so-called date, mainly because I didn't think she was interested in me. But then a few days later, one of our mutual friends from church called me. She told me Missy couldn't stop thinking about me. I didn't find out until several months later that the friend also called Missy that night and told her I really liked her! Neither one of us thought much about our fake date, but our friend decided to play matchmaker.

> I led Missy to the backyard and made my move. I planted a juicy lip lock on her, to which she responded enthusiastically.

The next time I saw Missy was at a youth meeting at the Kelletts' house. Oddly enough, Missy's family had lived in the same house for years until Mike and his family bought it. After the meeting I decided to check the credibility of our mutual friend who told me Missy was interested in me. We were outside and Missy was telling me stories of when she used to live there. I led her to the backyard and after she finished a story, I made my move. I turned and planted a juicy lip lock on her, to which she responded enthusiastically. I just wanted to see if she was interested in me and I got the answer. I have to admit I felt a spark or two during the encounter. It was nice!

Missy remembers a few more details of our early dating.

Missy: During our mock date, I also felt like we had a great time together. However, because we had mutually agreed to go out on this public-relations date, I would have never assumed anything more. I am not an aggressive person, and even though I felt something between us, I would have never made the first move! That's why, when Jason dropped me off, I just got out of the truck and went inside. He obviously hadn't asked me out because he thought I was pretty, funny, or interesting. In my mind, this was just business, whether I liked it or not. And I didn't like it. I was definitely attracted to him, but where I came from and the way I was raised, it was the boy's responsibility to make the first move. And he didn't, at least not that night. When my friend called me a few days later and told me that he liked me, I was surprised and thrilled! Little did I know that she'd done the same thing to Jason. The night after our first kiss at our youth minister's house, I remember trying not to get my hopes up. I knew about his reputation of dating as many girls as possible, and I thought there was a great chance that I would never hear from him again. However, I decided to go outside my comfort zone and give him a call.

One of his mom's friends answered the phone and when I asked to speak to Jason, she told me he was on his way to his girlfriend's house. I hung up, feeling dejected. About fifteen minutes later, he showed up at my house. I was the girlfriend!

We took our relationship really slow after that, but mainly because I lived twenty miles away. We mutually decided to pray together, and we made a decision to stop each other if we ever became too physical. The main things we discussed together were our relationship with Christ and how we could encourage our friends. Of course, it wasn't like it is today with cell phones, texting, and e-mails. I lived in the middle of nowhere and didn't have a car of my own, so it wasn't like I was talking to her every day or driving to town every night to see her. I really didn't see her much outside of church.

To be honest, I wasn't convinced our relationship would work. I had attended West Monroe High School, and Missy was a student at Ouachita Christian School. Her family was among the founders of OCS, which is a small private Christian school in Monroe. Her dad was a preacher, and her mother taught music at OCS. I was a country kid who went to a public school, and she was more of a middle-class girl who attended a private school. I was into hunting and fishing, and she liked drama and singing in the choir at school and church. Our lives up until that point were totally different. But Missy and I had a very deep spiritual connection, and I thought our mutual love for the Lord might be our biggest strength in sustaining our relationship. Even though Missy was so different from me, I found her world to be very interesting.

Looking back, perhaps another reason I decided to give our relationship a chance was because of my aunt Jan's bizarre premonition about Missy years earlier. My dad's sister Jan had helped bring him to the Lord, and she taught the fourth grade at OCS. One of her students was Missy, and they went to church together at White's Ferry Road Church. When I was a kid we attended a small church in the country, but occasionally we visited White's Ferry with my aunt Jan and her husband. One Sunday, Missy walked by us as we were sitting in the pew.

"Let me tell you something," Jan told me as she pointed at me and then Missy. "That's the girl you're going to marry."

Missy was nine years old. To say that was one of the dumbest things I'd ever heard would be an understatement. I love my aunt Jan, but she has a lot in common with her brother Si. They talk a lot, are very animated, and even seem crazy at times. However, they love the Lord and have great hearts. I actually never thought about it again until she reminded me of that day once Missy and I started getting serious. Freaky? A bit. Bizarre? Definitely! Was she right? Absolutely, good call!

> "Let me tell you something," Jan told me as she pointed at Missy. "That's the girl you're going to marry." Missy was nine years old.

Missy still isn't sure what my aunt Jan saw in her.

GOOD CALL

Missy: What did Jan see in me at nine years old? Well, you'll have to ask her about that. She was the only teacher in my academic history from whom I ever received a smack. She announced a rule to the class one day that no one could touch anyone else's possessions at any time (due to a recent rash of kids messing with other people's stuff). The next day, I moved some papers around on one of my classmates' desks before school, and he tattled on me. Because of her newly pronounced rule, she took me to the girls' bathroom and gave me a whack on the rear. At the time, I certainly would have never thought she had picked me out to marry her nephew!

The thing that really stood out about Missy was her independence, which is probably still her strongest characteristic today. She took so much abuse from her friends for dating me. She would often tell me stories about being asked why she was dating a redneck, backwoods hillbilly.

Missy: Jase did not fit the mold of the boys I was used to dating. Granted, I did not date very often, but I had been in an off-and-on relationship with a football player for over a year. The reason we would keep breaking up was because I wouldn't go further than a kiss with him. After a little while, he would come back, turn on his charm, and we would get back together. And the cycle would continue. October of 1987 was during one of these breakups. Once I went out with Jase, he was the only boy I thought about. When my old boyfriend came back around again and tried to convince me to get back together, I just wasn't interested anymore. My friends knew how I had always felt about him and couldn't understand why I wouldn't try again, instead of dating this "hick from West Monroe." I told them I just couldn't explain it. I was moving on and was so much happier. My good friends trusted my judgment and grew to like Jase, but the boys at school pretty much had one another's backs and gave me much grief. What did I care? I didn't know what smitten was until Jase. I was *smote*!

After high school, Missy attended the University of Louisiana–Monroe and was singing in the choir. She invited me to come listen to her sing in a concert. I had a fast-pitch softball game that night and went straight to the concert hall after my game. I was covered in dirt from head to toe, and although I didn't yet have a full beard, I hadn't shaved in several days. When I walked in, everybody else was spiffed up, wearing dresses and suits and ties. People were looking at me like, "Who is this ham?" I sat down and listened to the concert. They were singing songs that weren't even in English, and I thought it was terrible. But Missy was one of the best singers onstage, and I knew how much singing meant to her.

After the concert, Missy walked up to me and kissed me. I could feel eyeballs burning holes through me. I could sense everyone around us stopping and thinking, *What in the world is she doing with that guy?* It's a feeling I've had many times since that night. But Missy never seemed to care what others thought about us. It didn't bother her. However, it was difficult for me to believe that she would stay with me for the long haul when most people in her life were asking her why she was dating me. For both of us, it was always about our love for God and each other.

One of my many weaknesses as a young man was jealousy. I wasn't a very trusting person until I was about twenty-five years old. I had definitely been influenced negatively as a kid because my dad had trust issues, and friends and family members who had problems in their relationships had also soured me. I had a rule that if you were with me, you shouldn't even be alone with another guy. Since I didn't attend Missy's school, I didn't know if she was seeing other people or talking to other guys. While I was sharing my faith with the people on my list, I encountered this guy who was really quiet. He attended school with Missy at Ouachita Christian School. I shared the Gospel with him and baptized him.

It was difficult for me to believe that Missy would stay with me for the long haul.

"Hey, I want you to do me a favor," I told him. "Do you know Missy West?"

"Yeah, I've seen her around," he said.

"I want you to watch her at school and let me know what's going on," I said.

Well, this guy was so quiet that I forgot about asking him to spy on my girlfriend. A few months later, I saw him at youth church.

"Do you want to hear my report?" he asked me.

I could feel the blood rushing out of my body. He had a notebook in his hands, and I didn't like the way his body language looked. He acted like something bad was going on, so I figured my relationship with Missy was about to end. But his reports didn't reveal anything bad, and Missy was being very loyal. To my surprise, he had never seen her alone with another guy.

When I was about twenty-five, I made a decision to be my own man. I decided I wasn't going to worry about things that were out of my control or allow other people's bad decisions to affect my life. It was that simple. I put jealousy to death, and one of the reasons was what I found in 1 Corinthians 13:7, which says that love always trusts. Of course, when Missy found out about my clandestine snooping years later, she wasn't happy. It was hard for her to believe that I had really changed just because I made the decision to overcome my mistrustful tendencies. I believe it was because the Lord was working in me that I was able to make the change.

The year after I graduated from high school, I immediately went to work with my dad running a crawfish farm on our land. I got free room and board and a little gas money. The greatest benefit was getting to eat crawfish every day, but you talk about a hard way to make a dollar! We had about five hundred crawfish traps spread across our property, and we figured out that fresh bait was better than the artificial bait you could buy in bags. So we would catch fish from the river and use the trash fish for bait. We would wake up well before daylight and run the fishnets. We would send the good fish to the market, chop up the rest for bait, and then it was off to the crawfish nets.

We had a boat that was like a crawfish processing station. There was a table in the middle of the boat and it had a hole in the middle of it. We'd dump the trap into the boat and then sort the crawfish, tossing the old bait and other creatures through the hole. Usually, one out of every five traps had a snake in it—and one out of every ten snakes could kill you! After a while, we got good at spotting the venomous snakes in a trap, and that's the only thing that halted production—stopping to kill a cottonmouth water moccasin! The traps were spaced far enough apart that by the time you finished cleaning out one trap and filling it with bait again, you'd arrive at the next trap. By the end of the day, you were knee-deep in nonvenomous snakes and a lot of filth! Really, the worst part of operating a crawfish farm was that after about a month of fish fins poking you and crawfish pinching you, you'd have a bad case of blood poisoning. My hands would swell up, streaks would go up my arms, and I would end up in the hospital every few weeks.

But the money for the family was good, and we were eating crawfish every day. We figured out how to cook crawfish a hundred and one different ways. We were like Bubba from *Forrest*

Gump—we fried them, stewed them, boiled them, and they were all good. It's hard to mess up a crawfish. The worst thing you can do to crawfish is freeze them. Even though they'll still be edible, they'll lose their taste. I told you earlier that I've never mounted an animal in my life, but I wish we'd mounted the biggest crawfish we ever caught. We had a crawfish that was twice the size of any other crawfish I'd ever seen. It was as big as a lobster, and like an idiot, I ate him!

When crawfish weren't in season, I made money by roofing houses, guiding duck hunts, and cutting firewood with my friend Mike Williams. When Mike was a kid, his dad made him cut firewood for a living. In my opinion, he became the greatest lumberjack in Louisiana and perhaps the USA. Mike was as wide as a hundred-year-old oak and just as tall! He was a firewood-cutting machine! I teamed up with him and we were probably cutting and stacking six to eight cords of firewood a day. I'm talking about cutting down trees, sawing and splitting them up, and delivering them to customers! Fortunately, Mike was faster with an ax than I was with a chain saw.

> Once we caught a crawfish that was as big as a lobster, and like an idiot, I ate him!

At the time, I was driving a 1970 Ford truck that I'd bought for a thousand bucks. In my world, if a vehicle runs and has air in its tires, then it's worth a thousand dollars! The price never changes. I abused that truck for several years, only to sell it for a thousand bucks for an upgrade. It had a rebuilt hot rod engine and was fast! When we cut firewood in the rain, my truck would slide all over dirt roads and occasionally bounce off trees, so both of the truck's sides were badly dented. After a while, I couldn't open either door. It was real-life *Dukes of Hazzard*!

I remember the first time Missy approached the door and tried to open it. I told her the door wouldn't open, and she started to go around to the other side. I informed her that the other door didn't open, either. As she looked at me with a blank stare, I said, "Rule number one: if you want to go with me, you've got to crawl through the window."

On our second date, I picked up Missy at her house and told her we had to make a pit stop to pick up crawfish bait at the fish market. We'd figured out a way to speed up the process by using the fish market's gutbuckets instead of running nets ourselves. Through trial and error, we determined that the best crawfish bait was buffalo-fish heads. Unfortunately, when I pulled up to the market to get the garbage cans full of fish heads, I realized they had been outside for a couple of days. It was a warm day, and I could tell from the buzzing of hundreds of flies it was going to be nasty! I knew it was going to be the ultimate test of our relationship. The tubs were too heavy for one man to carry, so I told Missy, "I'm going to need your help on this." She crawled out the window, and I led her to the trash cans filled with buffalo heads waiting for us. Like an idiot, the first thing she did was open the lid of a trash can. Immediately, she started gagging and dry-heaving in the parking lot.

"Rule number two," I said. "Never pop the lid on a trash can."

> "Rule number one: if you want to go with me, you've got to crawl through the window."

ARRANGED DATE

Much to my surprise, Missy regained her composure and helped me load the trash cans into the back of my truck. Right then, I realized our relationship might work out. She was climbing through windows and hauling fish heads.

A few months into our relationship, we had a campout down at my dad's place. There were a lot of people from church, and we played games and fished into the night. We all gathered around a huge campfire, ate dinner, and sang songs together. Missy was clinging all over me, mainly because she was scared of everything flying in the air or crawling on the ground. It was one of those nights when you feel closer to God and everyone else because of the setting and the ambience—despite the bug activity. That was the first time we said "I love you" to each other. Now, there is still an ongoing debate as to who said it first. I remember clearly that she whispered, "I love you," and then I responded. She is convinced that I said it first, but she was under the influence of bug paranoia. I believe her condition affected her memory.

Missy and I became best friends, and soon after our first year together I decided to propose to her. It was a bit of a silly proposal. It was shortly before Christmas Day 1988, and I bought her a potted plant for her present. I know, I know, but let me finish. The plan was to put her engagement ring in the dirt (which I did) and make her dig to find it (which I forced her to do). I was then going to give a speech saying, "Sometimes in life you have to get your hands dirty and work hard to achieve something that grows to be wonderful." I got the idea from Matthew 13, where Jesus gave the Parable of the Sower. I don't know if it was the digging through the dirt to find the ring or my speech, but she looked dazed and confused. So I sort of popped the question: "You're going to marry me, aren't you?" She eventually said yes (whew!), and I thought everything was great.

A few days later, she asked me if I'd asked her dad for his blessing. I was not familiar with this custom or tradition, which led to a pretty heated argument about people who are raised in a barn or down on a riverbank. She finally convinced me that it was a formality that was a prerequisite for our marriage, so I decided to go along with it. I arrived one night at her dad's house and asked if I could talk with him. I told him about the potted plant and the proposal to his daughter, and he pretty much had the same bewildered look on his face that she'd had. He answered quite politely by saying no. "I think you should wait a bit, like maybe a couple of years," he said. I wasn't prepared for that response. I didn't handle it well. I don't remember all the details of what was said next because I was uncomfortable and angry. I do remember saying, "Well, you are a preacher so I am going to give you some scripture." I quoted 1 Corinthians 7:9, which says: "It is better to marry than to burn with passion." That didn't go over very well. I informed him that I'd treated his daughter with respect and he still wouldn't budge. I then told him we were going to get married with him or without him, and I left in a huff.

> I quoted the Bible to Missy's dad: "It is better to marry than to burn with passion." That didn't go over very well.

Over the next few days, I did a lot of soul-searching and Missy did a lot of crying. I finally decided that it was time for me to become a man. Genesis 2:24 says: "For this reason [creation of a woman] a man will leave his father and mother and be united to his wife, and they will become one flesh." God is the architect of marriage, and I'd decided that my family would have God as its foundation. It was time for me to leave and cleave, as they say. My dad told me once that my mom would cuddle us when we were in his nest, but there would be a day when it would be his job to kick me out. He didn't have to kick me out, nor did he have to ask me, "Who's a man?" Through prayer and patience, Missy's parents eventually came around, and we were more than ready to make our own nest.

7

---------- ◆ ----------

STRANGE CREATURES

APPRECIATING FROGS AND WOMEN

He who finds a wife finds what is good and receives
favor from the Lord.

—PROVERBS 18:22

My absolute favorite thing in the world to do is frog hunt-ing, and my favorite things to eat are fried frog legs. I've found that frogs are some of the strangest creatures on earth. Did you know frogs absorb water through their skin, so they don't need to drink? Frogs can lay as many as four thousand eggs at once, and in one species of frog, the male takes its mate's eggs into its mouth as soon as they show signs of life and keeps them there until they emerge as fully grown froglets! Some frogs can jump up to twenty times their own body length in a single leap, and frog bones form a new ring every year when the frog hibernates, just like a tree. Scientists count the rings to determine the age of a frog. When God created frogs, He made an exotic delicacy.

This might be a surprise to some people, but I like hunting frogs more than I like shooting ducks. A lot of people prefer frog gigging, but I've always used only my hands to catch frogs. In frog gigging, people use a four-or-five-tined gig to stab the frogs. I choose not to use a gig because a glancing blow can injure a frog without its being caught. I prefer "hand-to-frog" combat, which allows me to catch it—or it gets away for another try. I rarely miss one. When I go frog-hunting, not only do I try to think like a frog so I can find its hiding place, but I also physically act like a frog so I can catch it. If the frog jumps as I try to catch it, I jump along with it, no matter what I might be jumping into.

I think it's much more effective and way more fun than using a gig.

When I go frog hunting, not only do I try to think like a frog but I also physically act like a frog so I can catch it.

My buddy Mike Williams, the lumberjack, was my partner in crime when it came to frog hunting. He scouted the best frog-hunting holes around West Monroe and even made maps. We frog-hunted most ditches, creeks, rivers, bayous, and, yes, golf courses in North Louisiana. I feel bad to this day about all of Mike's equipment that I totally destroyed while pursuing frogs. I viewed it as collateral damage for being the best frog hunter you could possibly be. Mike always seemed to find a way to forgive me, and every time I thought I had lost him as a friend, he would come pulling up in my yard with a new rig. Mike thought frogs were so delicious he wanted to travel to Africa because he read that's where the biggest bullfrogs in the world are. He was actually right—the goliath frog from Cameroon in West

Africa grows to be one foot long. Its legs would look like king crab legs in a frying pan! We seriously discussed going but never did. Of course, we're not dead yet.

Mike discovered that the best bullfrogs in West Monroe were located in a pond on the fourteenth fairway of a private golf course. He cased the place for weeks from an adjacent neighborhood, and we waited for a stormy night. We figured no one would be out and about during a storm, and we didn't want to get caught on this swanky golf course. Our best route to the pond was parking at the end of a street on the edge of the neighborhood and carrying the boat by hand onto the golf course. The stormy night finally came and we parked my truck, got on each end of the boat, and made our way through cane thickets during a nasty thunderstorm. There was lightning and thunder as we made our way across the golf course, running with the boat and flashlights. The best way to catch a frog is to shine a flashlight in its eyes, which kind of stuns it, and then grab it quickly before the frog realizes what happened. We caught seventy-five frogs that night! We left our ice chest in the truck, so I was putting frogs in my socks and the pockets of my pants and shirt.

When we couldn't carry any more frogs, we made our way back to my truck. As soon as we arrived, police cars came from every direction. A homeowner in the neighborhood must have seen my truck and feared we were burglars. As the police questioned us, they must have thought Mike was drunk, because he couldn't stop laughing. They kept asking me what we'd been drinking and smoking and where it was. When a policeman shined a light on my shirt, I figured out what Mike was giggling about. I forgot I'd stuffed a frog into the front pocket of my shirt and buttoned it. Its legs were sticking out of my pocket and it looked like it was wearing a diaper! The police let us go but warned us to never sneak back onto the golf course because it was trespassing. We probably went back three or four times by a different route and never were caught.

Mike and I currycombed the countryside for places to frog-hunt. One night we found a ditch in the middle of nowhere and had the best frog hunt ever. We hunted all night and were so tired and hungry that we drove straight to a doughnut shop. We arrived thirty minutes before it opened, and after being informed they didn't open until six A.M., we decided to wait. We didn't say a word to each other as we took in the aroma of the fresh, hot doughnuts being prepared. We ordered a dozen each, but after we ate them so quickly we decided to do the same thing again. It was the perfect ending to an epic frog hunt, and it's one of the reasons I love hot doughnuts so much.

Catching frogs can take a toll on your body. I have repeatedly been battered and actually was knocked out cold when I dove headfirst into a cypress tree. One time, I jumped out of a boat to catch a frog in a thicket, and as I lunged to grab the frog, a purple poisonous thorn stuck me behind the ear. I vomited for three days and my face was badly swollen. If it had stuck me in the temple, I probably would have died. My greatest frog catch occurred after our boat ran aground. I saw the biggest bullfrog I've ever seen! The problem was, there were three snakes in between the frog and me: a cottonmouth water moccasin, a nonvenomous water snake, and then a bigger fish snake. Undeterred, I triple-jumped the three snakes and grabbed the frog in one swoop. Then I triple-jumped back the other way without getting bit. It probably wasn't the smartest thing I've ever done, but, hey, I got the frog!

I love frog hunting so much I actually skipped my high school graduation to go. I graduated from West Monroe High School in 1987, but I didn't actually receive my diploma until many years later. I really didn't see the point of having an event to declare that I'd graduated. Plus, the cost of buying a cap and gown was ridiculous! You want to dress me up in a cap and gown, say I graduated, and make me pay for it? Yeah, right. I thought my money would be better spent on something like fishing lures or ammo. In an act of rebellion, I persuaded one of my buddies to go frog-hunting with me on graduation night. We caught over a hundred and fifty frogs on the Ouachita River, and I felt it was one of the best decisions I'd ever made. I know it was way more fun than walking across a stage to receive my diploma.

Many years later, after much encouragement from Missy, I wheeled into the parking lot of West Monroe High School, walked into the principal's office, and asked a young woman for my diploma. She walked into a back room and returned with a stack of dusty diplomas. As she thumbed through them, I felt a sense of pride that there were obviously a few more frog hunters from my high school than I realized. The lady handed me my diploma, and I jokingly offered her an apology for being a little late but thanked her for not throwing it away.

While frogs are some of the strangest creatures on earth, they can't hold water against women. One of my dad's favorite sayings when we were kids was "Boys, when God made a woman He made a strange creature." I wasn't married for very long before I realized he was right.

Missy and I were married on August 10, 1990. To say our marriage got off to a rocky start would be an understatement. My brothers and closest friends took me frog-hunting the night before my wedding for my bachelor party. As we were searching for frogs, my oldest brother, Alan, gave me a lot of advice on marriage in general as we motored along the bayou. The main thing he reminded me of is that God is the architect of marriage. Having a great relationship with our Creator is the best thing you can do for your marriage relationship. Alan gave me an illustration of a triangle with the husband and wife on the bottom corners and God at the top corner. His point was that as each person moves closer to God, they also move closer to each other. I never forgot that and he was right. I was mainly the motorman that night and was filled with anxiety in anticipation of the wedding. As we moved along, we saw two big frogs mating on the riverbank.

"Whoa, there you go!" Al shouted.

It kind of broke the ice for a conversation about intimacy and sex. Missy and I had not seen each other much in the previous couple of months because we couldn't keep our hands off each other. Many times we had to remind each other of our commitment to stay pure and had had many prayers together. We were not perfect, but one of us would always stop things from getting too heated. Eventually, we decided to have only a long-distance relationship via telephone and our face-to-face encounters became limited to church and public gatherings. As our wedding was approaching, Missy and I were both a little bit nervous about having sex for the first time. I think that's the way it is when you're both virgins. We were both excited because we'd decided to save ourselves for marriage and our big night was finally here!

I remember standing at the front of the church auditorium when Missy came out in her white wedding dress. Before that moment I was really nervous and was thinking about whether I was actually ready to get married. But then I melted when I saw her. She looked more gorgeous than ever, and I felt a sense of calm come over me. The ceremony was great, and as it went along I think we both became even more anxious about our first night together. After we left our wedding reception, I asked Missy what she wanted to do. I was pretty much ready to see what I had been missing.

"Well, I'm hungry," she said.

We went to a burger joint, and as we ate I could tell she was nervous about what was going to transpire. We'd planned to stay in a hotel the night of our wedding and fly to Hawaii the next day for our honeymoon. I'll be perfectly honest: our first night together was more of an exploratory expedition into the human anatomy than a blissful adventure. It felt like a biology experiment. Missy doesn't care for the way I describe it, but that's what happens when neither one of you has had sex before. You find your way through it and figure out what's going on. Then you go from there, and it becomes much more enjoyable.

I remember meeting a man who gave sex seminars to students at various college campuses. To get people to come he passed out flyers that were entitled "How to Have the Best Sex on Earth." Of course, his lecture attracted a huge turnout. He spoke about sex between two virgins on their wedding night being disease-free, guilt-free, comparison-free, and shame-free, as well as being pleasing to God. It is the best sex you can have on earth. He explained that many people fall short and that is why Jesus died on a cross. In Christ anyone can start over. As 1 Corinthians 6:9–11 says: "The sexually immoral . . . will [not] inherit the kingdom of God. And that is what some of you were. But you were washed . . . sanctified . . . [and] justified in the name of the Lord Jesus Christ and by the Spirit of our God." The forgiveness found in Christ doesn't take away from the fact that God's way is always the best way for a marriage and our world. Hebrews 13:4 says: "Marriage should be honored by all, and the marriage bed kept pure." That is exactly what Missy and I did.

I'll be perfectly honest: our first night together was more of an exploratory expedition into the human anatomy than a blissful adventure.

As awkward as our first night together was, our honeymoon was even worse. As soon as we arrived in Hawaii, I became ill with strep throat. I mostly slept and lay in the bathtub in our hotel room for a week shaking violently with a fever. Missy looked out the window at the beautiful beach and Pacific Ocean and cried. It was miserable. I was sweating profusely and thought I was going to die. We'd saved our money for months—about eight hundred dollars—to go to Hawaii, and it ended up being the worst trip of our lives. My getting sick actually saved us from the embarrassment of realizing that we couldn't do much on eight hundred bucks anyway. We laugh now at being so naive and young. When we went back to Hawaii for the season finale of *Duck Dynasty* last year, Missy was determined to make up for a lot of bad memories. I did everything she wanted to do. We went on helicopter rides, boat rides, romantic dinners, and everything else you could do in Hawaii. She got her money's worth the second time!

Missy cried during our first week of marriage because I was so sick, and I couldn't blame her because my illness wrecked our honeymoon. But after we went home to West Monroe, I woke up on the twenty-eighth day of our marriage, and she was crying again! I realized then that I had a few things to learn about marriage. You're living in a different environment, you're away from your parents for the first time in your life, and you're sharing a bed and home with someone new. It's a different life than what you had when you were single, when you could get up and leave if things got tough. More than anything else, women are generally more emotional than men. When I give newlyweds in our church advice, I tell them, "Look, when you wake up on day thirty of your marriage and she's crying for no reason, don't panic. It's normal. It's going to happen. Most women are going to cry from time to time. It's the way God made them."

One of the biggest adjustments for Missy during the early part of our marriage was her husband's being away from home so much. During duck-hunting season, I was gone from about four o'clock in the morning until dark. One of the great things about Missy is her independence, and she immediately realized that I needed my space. She knew I wasn't going to find another woman in the woods. She knew I wasn't doing anything wrong. She realized it was good, clean fun, and that's why she has always encouraged me to do it. In all the years we've been together, she has never raised her voice or complained about my hunting or fishing.

Of course, Missy had to get over her initial fears about the dangers of hunting. I gave her a set of rules early in our marriage. I told her, "Look, if I go hunting before daylight, you can expect me back at dark. I might come back at noon, but don't panic unless it's an hour after dark and I'm not home yet. If I go frog-hunting or scouting for ducks at night, don't expect me back until daylight. If it's an hour after daylight and I'm not home yet, then you might ought to call somebody." I told her there was some risk involved with hunting, but I didn't want her calling every hour wondering where I was and what I was doing.

> Missy realized hunting was good, clean fun, and that's why she has always encouraged me to do it.

Now, there were a couple of times in my life when I wished she'd called. One time, I was alone in rising backwater caused by the Ouachita River flooding on my dad's property and was going too fast in a boat. The water level was high, and it's easy to lose your trail. I tried to jump a big fallen tree and the boat went airborne. I landed between two saplings and was stuck! My motor was out of the water and it was screaming! I spent a few hours between those trees. I found a piece of knife in the boat and began to whittle down the trees to release the boat. I knew Missy wouldn't be worried about me until after dark, and right before dark I got out from between the trees. Of course, I was lost and didn't know where I was. I eventually made it home before Missy called Phil for help.

Another time I was hunting squirrels at Tensas, which was one of my dad's favorite hunting spots. I was on foot, and somehow, I got turned around and came out eight miles down the road in the wrong direction. During the journey back to camp, I had an up-close encounter with a Louisiana black bear that I managed to get away from. I walked all night, and when I finally reached our camp right before daylight, Phil was gone! He had forgotten I was with him and was already gone for the next day's hunt. Missy was worried sick but refrained from having the Louisiana National Guard out looking for me.

During duck season I would leave before daylight, and Missy would often get upset because I'd forget to turn off the carport lights. It was about the only thing she nagged me about. One morning, I got up to leave to go hunting and it was raining. I'd backed my truck into our carport the night before to load up my hunting gear. As I pulled away, I looked in my rearview mirror and saw that I'd left the light on again. I jumped out of my truck and ran into the carport to turn the light off. As I turned back to run to my truck, I realized I'd put the gearshift in reverse instead of park! As the truck was racing backward, the open door hit Missy's Pontiac Grand Am and bent the door back. I jumped on Missy's car, dove into my truck, and slammed it into park.

Sitting there among crumpled metal and shattered glass, I pondered what to do next. I couldn't go in reverse because there was a big hill behind our carport. I was pinned between the side of the house and her car. I decided that since I'd already wrecked the driver's side of her car, I was going out the way I came in. I put my truck in drive and swiped her car again on the way out. I was determined to go duck-hunting no matter what! The problem was that my door wouldn't shut and was barely hanging on to the frame of my truck. I drove on the shoulder of the road the entire way to Phil's house.

> I jumped on Missy's car, dove into my truck, and slammed it into park.

About a mile and a half from Phil's house, I turned a corner and there was an eight-point buck standing in the middle of the road! Boom! I hit the deer head-on, and it flipped over my truck. I thought it was going to hit the windshield. Fortunately, it hit the hood of my truck and bounced over the cab. I climbed out of my truck and immediately smelled antifreeze pouring out of my busted radiator. One of my buddies who was going hunting with us pulled up behind me. He helped me throw the dead deer into the back of my truck and then followed me to Phil's house. Phil and my brothers were already on four-wheelers ready to go to the duck blind.

"What in the world happened?" Phil asked me. "Did you flip your truck?"

"It's a long story," I said. "Let's go duck-hunting."

We ended up having one of our best duck hunts of the season. When we returned to Phil's house, I filled up about twenty bottles of water. My busted radiator leaked the entire way home, and I had to stop every couple of miles to fill it up with water. There was a body shop close to our house, so I pulled in there before going home.

"Well, whatcha think?" I asked the mechanic.

"Well, we can fix it," he said. "I can get you a radiator."

"What's it going to cost me?" I asked.

"Well, what are you going to do with the deer?" he said. "I can get you a radiator for the deer."

About that time, the mechanic's assistant walked up to my truck.

"What are you going to do with the rack of horns?" the assistant asked me.

"Hey, if you can fix my door so it will close, you can have the horns," I told him.

There's nothing quite like good, old-fashioned redneck bartering. Unfortunately, I didn't get off so easy with the damage to Missy's car. In all the excitement of the day, I'd completely forgotten to tell her that I'd wrecked her car. When I got home, she told me somebody pulled in the driveway and sideswiped it. I couldn't tell a lie.

"You remember how you scolded me about forgetting to turn out the carport light?" I said.

"Yeah," she said.

"Well, this is what happens when you start worrying about small things like that," I said.

A big argument ensued, but Missy took her car to the body shop, and it cost us several hundred dollars to fix it. Two days after we picked up her car, I was driving it to Phil's house. Wouldn't you know it? Another deer jumped in front of me in the road. I totaled Missy's car. We had to buy her a new car, and my truck never drove the same after it was wrecked, either. I sold it for—you guessed it—a thousand bucks.

By the second or third year of our marriage, Missy had pretty much adapted to my peculiarities—or at least most of them. After one late-night frog hunt, I came home and skinned the frogs in the kitchen. I left them on ice in the sink and climbed into bed. When Missy saw the frogs in the sink later that morning, she literally passed out! She thought I was a barbaric mountain man for eating frogs, and she could never stomach even tasting them—at least not until I tricked her into eating them!

I have always enjoyed the process of catching, cleaning, and cooking my food. In my family, cooking has always been an honorable thing, with some people having more of a talent for it than others. Since Missy's parents were on the road a lot as missionaries, they rarely cooked at home. Missy's mother never taught her how to cook. So from the very beginning of our marriage, I told Missy I would do the cooking—but she wanted to learn how. One morn-

When Missy saw the frogs in the sink later that morning, she literally passed out!

ing, she even called Kay and asked her how long you have to cook an egg before it's soft. "What are you talking about?" Kay asked her. "You do know you have to remove the shell from the egg, don't you?"

One night, before Missy came home from work, I made a batch of my world-famous sautéed frog legs. I got the recipe from a Cajun man from South Louisiana on a duck-hunting trip. I soaked the legs in lemon juice, battered them in flour, and then cooked them in butter in a frying pan. When Missy walked into the kitchen, I told her, "Taste this."

She took a bite. "That's the best thing I've ever tasted!" she said. "How did you get chicken to taste like that?"

"It's not chicken," I told her. "You just ate a frog."

The frog legs tasted so good that she wasn't very upset with me for tricking her into eating them. For the first few years of our marriage, Missy refused to eat venison because she didn't want to eat Bambi. Now she loves deer steak. She said she could never eat dove because they were so peaceful, but now she loves them, especially when they're wrapped in bacon and stuffed with cream cheese and jalapeño peppers. I used to have to pick the meat off the bones for her, but now she eats it right off the bone! She also couldn't stand the smell of fish, but now she loves mustard-fried or blackened crappie.

While Missy has acquired a taste for frog legs, she still doesn't understand my fascination with catching them. One night after church, we were stopped at an intersection while driving home. Our two sons, Reed and Cole, and our daughter, Mia, were in

Missy's car with us. It was raining, and I saw one of the biggest bullfrogs I've ever seen sitting in the middle of the road. I put her car in park.

"What are you about to do, Jason?" Missy asked me.

"I'm going to catch that frog," I said. "Y'all want to flag traffic for me?"

"Don't you dare get out of this car," she said.

Before she could finish her sentence, I'd jumped out of the driver's seat and was maneuvering my way to the frog. I moved toward the back of it, assumed the frog position, and then leaped on him! Missy and Mia were screaming in the car, and my boys were laughing. As I got back in the car, I explained to everyone that I probably saved that frog's life by catching him at a busy intersection. I held the frog in one hand and drove with the other the entire way home.

When I walked into the kitchen, Missy asked me, "What are you fixing to do?"

I cleaned the frog on the kitchen table and fried its legs in a frying pan.

"I can't believe you just did that," Missy said. "I thought you saved his life."

Hey, but I gave him a noble death.

Despite our differences, Missy and I built a foundation for our marriage in Christ. Before we were married, we were mocked by some of our friends and acquaintances for being virgins. I remember one of my friends constantly belittling me and saying I needed to experience sex before marriage just to know what to do and how to do it. I saw him years later and quickly told him, "I've got three kids. I figured it out."

Marriage is about so much more than sex. It takes a lot of work on a daily basis to have a successful relationship. Missy and I are spiritual partners and best friends, despite the constant changing of circumstances. I have realized that my dad was right, women are strange, but the differences we have keep life interesting. The righteous acts we commit in overcoming our differences are what make marriage exciting. It does not matter to me where we live or what we drive; what matters is the person I have chosen to be with and how long we reside together. My number one goal in life is to help my wife and kids get to heaven, where we plan to live together as part of a forever family. While we are on this earth I try to live out on a daily basis the words of Joshua 24:15: "But as for me and my household, we will serve the Lord."

8

––––––⟡––––––

RAINOUT

Declare his glory among the nations, his marvelous
deeds among all peoples.

—PSALM 96:3

As a duck hunter there is no greater satisfaction than calling in a bunch of ducks and shooting all of them. It doesn't happen very often. We try to get the ducks in as close as we can, so we can wipe every one of them out with a volley of gunfire. There is a method to our madness, though, because the more we shoot out of a bunch, the fewer ducks we disturb. The faster the hunting party can get away from the duck hole, the better the chance you have for a good hunt the next day. Ducks are smart, and it usually doesn't take much for them to become wary of duck blinds and decoys.

Through the years, us Duckmen have become famous for our "rainouts" on our hunting DVDs. "Rainout" is a term we coined as hunters, and it happens on the rare occasions when the majority of the ducks, if not the whole bunch, fall from the sky. Rainouts are the indelible moments that have become stories we relive over and over. Of course, our quest for perfection in duck hunting causes daily debates about what went wrong and who should be blamed. We've had arguments that lasted for years, especially between Uncle Si and me, but it's all in good fun. Last year during teal season, the first bunch of the year came in perfectly to our decoy spread after some timely calling. There were six of us in the blind, and we each shot three times—shooting multiple ducks per shot. There were twenty-three teals in the bunch, and we shot every one of them! None got away. It was probably the best whacking of a bunch we've ever captured on film.

The only thing in life that gives me more of an adrenaline rush than a massive rainout is watching someone put their faith in Jesus Christ. And when it comes to salvation in Christ, I don't want a single one to get away. When I discovered who Jesus was, what He does for me, and what He will do, I was filled with an incredible desire to make it known to everyone. Duck hunting brings temporary enjoyment and delicious table fare, but Christ brings an eternal joy and real meaning to life. The joy I found in Christ led me to make a decision to dedicate two years of my life to studying God's Word at a seminary in my hometown.

During the two years before Missy and I were married, I attended the White's Ferry Road Church School of Biblical Studies and graduated the month before our wedding. Missy had planned on attending Abilene Christian University in Abilene,

Texas, which was her parents' alma mater. One of the biggest reasons her parents were initially opposed to our getting married so young—I was twenty-one and Missy was nineteen—was that they really wanted her to go to a Christian college. Missy told her dad that she knew the only reason he wanted her to go there was to find a Christian husband. She didn't understand why she needed to go because she'd already found one in West Monroe. What was I? A potted plant?

In the back of my mind, I thought going to "preaching school," as I called it, could possibly lead me to transfer to Abilene Christian University as a junior, if Missy and I decided to go there together. Plus, my going to preaching school sounded pretty good to her parents, who still weren't quite sure about me. Another reason I decided to attend seminary was because my older brother, Alan, was going there, too. Even though I attended White's Ferry Road Church, to say I didn't fit in at its seminary would be a massive understatement. To be honest, I stuck out like a smooth-faced man in a duck blind. Al is a bookworm and is kind of nerdy. Conversely, I'm not a big fan of reading or studying, unless I'm forced to do it. Even worse, the seminary had a pretty strict dress code, which I nonetheless constantly violated.

Since I'm an outdoors type of guy, it didn't take me long to become frustrated at seminary. I hate being cooped up in a room with no windows (it's the same problem I currently have with the duck call shop), especially during hunting season! I actually

In seminary, I stuck out like a smooth-faced man in a duck blind.

learned how to sleep with my eyes open in some of the more boring lectures. To break up the monotony, I ended up becoming the class clown and troublemaker. I constantly argued with instructors and fellow classmates. My main point of conflict was that I felt sometimes we studied the Bible as a legal document instead of a letter from God. I'm still convinced my point of view was correct, but I did a terrible job of communicating it. In fact, I nearly started several fights with my classmates. Our classes lasted from eight o'clock in the morning to four o'clock in the afternoon, five days a week. During duck season, I got up very early to hunt before going to class, and then I went back to the blind as soon as classes were over. By the end of the school day, I was itching to get out of there! Well, one day this guy asked a question at four P.M. Then he asked a follow-up question after the bell rang.

"Hey, why don't you shut up?" I told him.

Well, three guys met me in the parking lot after school. They were trying to rebuke me in a godly way for being rude. I responded with a misuse of Galatians 2:9: "How about I give you my right hand of fellowship?" Fortunately, they overlooked my anger, we resolved our differences in a Christian manner, and there were no fisticuffs. More than anything, seminary taught me a lot about discipline and commitment. In a lot of ways, it was a mental marathon. I studied Greek, Hebrew, English, and grammar, along with several classes in the Bible, history, world culture, and religion. The workload was extremely strenuous, and it was very difficult. It was like a spiritual boot camp. I would have never made it without Al's help and encouragement. Of course, he passed with flying colors, but I had to work extremely hard to graduate. We formed a special bond as brothers because we spent so much time studying together and encouraging each other.

Finishing seminary gave me a lot of confidence. It helped me get over my fear of public speaking because we were required to give so many presentations in front of our classmates. Graduating from seminary was a significant accomplishment for a guy who never really liked school. Somehow, I made it through two years of studies, despite spending an inordinate amount of time in the dean's office.

In spite of my rebellious tendencies, my church elders knew I loved the Lord, and they offered me a position as a paid intern. I accepted. Because the pay was minimal, I had to supplement my income in other areas. Along with helping my dad build duck calls, I chopped wood with Mike Williams and worked for a roofer, while Missy worked full-time for a local doctor's office. When we decided that I would take the position at our church, it meant that she had to forget her ideas about going to college and help support us financially. We were making enough money to pay our bills, but it was killing me physically. I knew I had to find something else to do, or I wasn't going to live very long. On top of that, we were spending as much time as we could bringing people closer to the Lord. Like a lot of young couples, the start of our marriage wasn't easy, but our early obstacles didn't have anything to do with money. Perhaps the main reason the

> Perhaps the main reason the first year of my marriage was so bumpy was because I rarely saw my wife.

first year of my marriage was so bumpy was because I rarely saw my wife.

Our ministry work began shortly after we returned to West Monroe from our honeymoon. Blake Gaston, my best friend from high school, was one of my groomsmen and was the only non-Christian in our wedding party. We had a bunch of wedding showers and other parties leading up to the wedding, and he attended most of them. I had already tried sharing the Gospel with him a couple of years earlier, and I remember sitting back and watching him, wondering if being around so many Christians was having a positive influence on him. About a week after we returned from our honeymoon, Blake called me and asked me to go fishing, which was his code for wanting to hear more about Christ. Blake was the first person I baptized. From there, it was like a domino effect.

We studied the Bible with so many people, including many I didn't even know. Missy and I baptized more than a hundred people in the first year of our marriage. Many of the people were my friends from high school. We would baptize one of my buddies, and then we'd baptize his girlfriend, her sister, her brother, and the rest of his family. It kind of blossomed once we started. It became a movement of people changing their lifestyles and declaring, "Jesus is Lord." Christ's message was constantly being shared.

For all the good work we were doing, our ministry was really straining our marriage. After a while, Missy was very frustrated.

RAINOUT

Missy: I worked in a doctor's office from eight A.M. to six P.M. every day. On most days I was home in time to cook supper for us. After dinner, either people would show up for Bible study or Jase would meet them in town. Most of our mentoring and "mission work" got cranked up around eight P.M. The people we were ministering to had former lifestyles that consisted of partying and staying out until all hours of the night and then sleeping away most of the day. Even though these new Christians were trying to change their lives, we realized it was going to take some time to change their behavioral patterns. Jase felt like he needed to be around them to help them stay out of trouble during those long nights. And most of those nights would result in additional Bible studies with new people he met while he was out. I remember many mornings when he would come home and crawl into bed about the time my alarm was going off. Many evenings were spent in

> *I knew in my head that we were doing this all for God, but my heart longed for my husband.*

our apartment studying the Bible with people or just entertaining them. Ultimately, this began to put a strain on our marriage. We didn't have a lot of time to be together because of our commitment to the people we were trying to help, and it ended up being a big sacrifice for both of us. I knew in my head that we were doing this all for God, but my heart longed for my husband.

Despite the difficulties and extreme fatigue that accompanied dealing with so many people, I witnessed the power of the message working. I like to think that much of our ministry was focused on relationships. If you love people and care about them, the greatest gift you can give them is eternal life with God. There were several times where the message had a profound effect on people I didn't even know. One night, I was at the house of a guy I didn't know and was sharing the Gospel with a guy I had only recently met, Kevin McIntosh. Kevin, just happened to show up at the house, but he seemed freaked out that we were having a Bible study there. Apparently, the house was a local gathering spot where they played video games and partied. When Kevin arrived at the house, I asked him if he wanted to sit in on the study, but he emphatically declined. He went into the next room and played video games while the rest of us talked. I passionately shared God's saving grace through Jesus Christ. But the guy I was talking to did not seem interested whatsoever, so I left to go to Wednesday-night church.

As I was walking to my truck, Kevin walked out of the house.

"Hey, I'm ready," he said.

"Ready for what?" I asked him.

"I was listening to your little study," he said. "I've never heard that before. I'm ready to get in on that."

"Well, climb into the truck," I said.

I took Kevin to church with me and quizzed him about his lifestyle, but mainly I wanted to see if he really understood what I had just shared. I was stunned by how much scripture he had retained and his love for Christ in such a short time. I felt indescribable excitement as I witnessed how the power of the message had cut his heart. He was baptized later that night.

A clean-shaven Phil from the mid-1970s, right after our family moved to the river. Phil made that old wooden boat himself.

Since I come from a family that doesn't take a lot of pictures, this is the earliest photo of me (1972) that I know of. Showing Alan, me, Miss Kay, and Phil.

Me around first or second grade. I had just learned how to use a comb and was so proud of my hair.

At my birthday party. That's my granny in the background and me looking at the camera as I stuff my face with cake—though Willie is the champion cake eater now. He's the other one stuffing his face.

A flood hit West Monroe around 1979, so naturally we took the opportunity to go fishing right up under my grandmother's house. Of course, we had no adult supervision. That's me standing up; Willie's in the middle next to one of our neighborhood friends.

My football picture from the fifth or sixth grade. I was on the community team and never showed up for practice because I never could catch a ride, but they let me play in the games because I was the fastest.

Me in about the seventh grade at Pinecrest Middle School. I was the shortest kid on the basketball team, so I worked to excel at the long-range shots—hey, it worked!

Here I am with my cousin playing dominoes. Well, I wasn't actually playing, but my cousin was placing the dominoes down too gently. I had to jump in and show him the proper domino-slamming technique.

Taking a ride in the cool green Jeep. That's me in the back with a random couple. Phil was driving, and Miss Kay held Jep in her lap, with Willie beside her.

Jep and I with our dog Gabe—my best buddy. When Gabe was older, he saved Jep's life when Jep wandered out too deep in the river. I was about eleven years old when I caught this giant catfish.

Me out by the cook shack in front of Phil's place. We actually cooked things out there—we had a fish fryer, a grill, and a smoker. Out in front you see a bunch of decoys, and I'm picking a duck.

Me as an intern at White's Ferry Road Church right after high school. This was one of those self-discovery times in my life, and I quickly discovered I didn't want to be cooped up in an office.

The guys out on an air boat in the winter of 1987. That's me in the middle with the Mickey Mouse ears. This is a rare photo of Alan *(right)* with a beard and me without one. I was still courting Missy, so I kept my face clean for her. But that soon changed.

I had proposed to Missy not too long before this photo was taken. She was a senior in high school and I was twenty. I had my best handsome-dude face on to impress my girl.

I walked up the aisle with a smirk on my face, dreaming about the honeymoon. Missy seems pretty happy about what was coming, too.

Me and my dapper-looking groomsmen. (*Back row, left to right*) My good friend W. E. Phillips; my frog-hunting partner in crime Mike Williams; me—the man of the hour; my good friend Rovance Lewis; the first guy I converted to Christ, Blake Gaston; Al on his knee, sporting a mullet. (*Front row, left to right*) A young Jep; Missy's cousin Chris; and Willie, doing his best to look debonair.

This is Missy in our second year of marriage and the beginnings of our Robertson family tradition of annual vacations together. Missy had to learn early on that if she was going to be married to an outdoors guy like me, alligators would be a part of her life. I was in the pond hunting for frogs.

This was a typical scene in 1996 after we bought our first house on Swiss Street, as we shared together in Bible study.

I was actually Duck Commander's first paid employee. Here I am looking less than happy, happy, happy because I was overworked and underpaid. I needed more help!

In the early days (around 2004), the Duck Commander business and workshop was at Phil's place. We've always tested every call we make—even from the start—and I always prided myself on my organizational skills. You can see the insulation on the wall next to me—we never did finish the place out. Years later, Miss Kay turned this building into a playhouse for the grandchildren—pretty cool.

Christmas morning, early 1990s, and fresh from the hunt. Phil and I are peeling shrimp in the kitchen and preparing to make crawfish pie.

At Gulf Shores, Alabama, the redneck beach, in 2005, with me looking kind of studly. We'd just finished hunting season, and it was a tradition back then to shave our beards every year once we got to the beach.

Here's a first picture of me as a dad with Reed right after he was born. I must have been thinking, "Well, I'm a father now. I sure did enjoy the process, but I'm now learning the reality of what comes after."

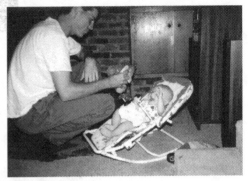

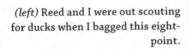

(left) My little guy Reed, around age four or five, caught his first fish at a family outing at Camp Ch-Yo-Ca—a Christian camp outside West Monroe.

(right) Reed with his first duck and the BB gun he used to shoot it. A proud little guy.

(left) Reed and I were out scouting for ducks when I bagged this eight-point.

(right) In Louisiana parents have to teach their children how to "read" alligators. Here Reed, age eleven, showed us what not to do.

Our Gulf Shores family photo, summer 2004. Holidays and Gulf Shores are the only times I cooperate with organized photos. The Robertsons have been going to this beach for more than twenty years now.

(left) In 2007 down at Gulf Shores, Alabama, we learned to fish for red fish. When I asked four-year-old Mia what she was thinking in this photo, she said, "Oh brother! That fish is bigger than me!"

(right) The next day I caught this near record-breaking red fish. He weighed around thirty-five to forty pounds.

This is what happens when the mother of your children is a yuppie—posed pictures. Mia, Reed, and Cole had to put up with it but not me. I had to apologize to the kids for the setup.

Here's my Mia with her cute smile after one of her surgeries in the summer of 2009 at a school event.

Me motoring alone in a boat right in front of Phil's house. It was freezing that day, but I still went hunting. That old, empty camp house in the background was often the target of our boyhood mischief. My brothers and I used to drive golf balls across the river and try to hit it.

Missy sang the national anthem at the 2011 Class A Championship game in the New Orleans Superdome, with Cole and Reed by her side.

This year Reed made his first touchdown at the same game Mia sang the national anthem. I was one proud papa.

Here's our Duck Commander Little League Dream Team. We were the 2012 league champions. Cole was on the team *(sixth from left in the back row)*. Four of us were coaches that year: Justin Martin standing next to Paul Stevens *(in the back left)* and I'm on the right end. Jay Stone, also a coach, is not pictured.

Here was a guy none of us really knew, but through a chance encounter he overheard the Gospel through a wall while playing games. It changed his entire life. He had no previous religious background or Christian friends before that night. That is some serious power! Kevin became one of my closest friends, and he became more like family. First Corinthians 1:17 says: "For Christ did not send me to baptize, but to preach the gospel—not with words of human wisdom, lest the cross of Christ be emptied of its power." We point people to Jesus, but God opens the heart for one to respond. Once Kevin heard it, he underwent a complete transformation. He called his friends and told them about it, and every time I turned around he was there. Kevin was a very good athlete and was great at about every sport or game he played, which came in handy as we were sharing God's Word with others. If we weren't hosting Bible studies or some other function at our house, I was usually with a group of guys at a pool hall. We would go and have as much fun as everyone else, but the difference was we were sober. One of the things that helped my relationships with those we were reaching out to was that I was not afraid to go to rough places or hang out with people who were cutting up. We were looking for opportunities to share the message with people who wouldn't be caught in a church—unless they were wheeled in via a casket! Matthew 11:19 says this of Jesus: "The Son of Man came eating and drinking, and they say, 'Here is a glutton and a drunkard, a friend of tax collectors and "sinners."'" Jesus didn't get that kind of reputation from hanging out only in temples and church buildings. Going to a bar or pool hall doesn't mean you're a drunk, just like sitting in a henhouse doesn't make you a chicken. It's the same in the opposite setting. Sitting in a church building doesn't make you a follower of Christ. In fact, Acts 17:24 says: "The God who made the world and everything in it is the Lord of heaven and earth and does not live in temples built by hands." God lives in heaven and in the hearts of men and women on earth. Misunderstanding this principle is one of the reasons so many people act one way in a church building and the total opposite everywhere else.

One night, Kevin and I were at a pool hall where we saw a guy playing pool by himself; this guy looked like a hustler. He asked me if I wanted to play for twenty dollars.

"I'll tell you what," I told him. "You can play my buddy Kevin. If you win two out of three games, I'll give you twenty dollars. If he wins, you have to leave with us and go to a Bible study."

The guy looked at me like I was nuts. He walked around the pool table a few times, pondering my offer. I took a twenty-dollar bill out and placed it on the table.

"Okay," he said. "Let's do it."

What he didn't know was that Kevin is quite the player and that I don't make bets with eternal consequences on the line unless I know we're going to win! Of course, my buddy Kevin beat him. In fact, Kevin broke and ran the table in two straight games. The other guy never even took a shot! To my surprise, the guy followed through on his bet, although he didn't seem too happy about it. As we walked to my truck to leave, he threw a full can of beer across the road and declared he was ready for a change in his life anyway. I thought that was a powerful statement since he didn't even know what we were going to share with him. He knew how we rolled, despite our presence in such a rugged place. We stud-

> He threw a full can of beer across the road and declared he was ready for a change in his life.

ied the Bible with him for several hours and baptized him the same night. What I didn't know was that the guy was sentenced to prison for an earlier crime the very next day! I wouldn't see him again until he showed up unannounced with his Bible in hand at my house on Christmas Day a couple of years later.

"Hey, I just got out of jail," he told me.

"Did they let you out or did you escape?" I asked him.

"I was released," he said.

He then tearfully thanked me for sharing with him and let me know that was the best thing that could have happened to him before the two years of prison. Obviously, neither one of us believed our encounter had been an accident. He came to our church a couple of times over the next few months, and I continued to study with him. After a while, though, he quit coming around and I lost track of him.

Missy and I lived in an apartment for about eight months after we were married. Then we moved into a small two-bedroom house on Swiss Street in West Monroe, which is near White's Ferry Road Church. Missy found the house in the foreclosure listings, and I never saw it until after we signed the documents to buy it. I put into practice my idea that it doesn't matter what kind of structure you live in. I think we paid thirty thousand dollars for the house. It was old and small, but it was our first home together, and it was where we lived when our oldest son, Reed, was born.

Our first house is where I learned the true meaning of "love your neighbor." On one side of us were three guys who seemingly stayed drunk twenty-four hours a day. I preached Jesus to them one day, only to get threatened and cussed out. I ended up putting up a privacy fence because they were so loud and vile. Some of the people I shared Jesus with were initially met through confrontations. There was a very large man in our neighborhood who walked through our backyard daily. He was probably six feet tall and weighed more than four hundred pounds. He was a giant man! He lived behind us and kept walking through our yard to go drink beer with my other neighbors. After a couple of weeks of watching the guy, I confronted him by yelling across my yard.

"Hey, you need to walk around my house," I told him. "Stay out of my backyard."

The guy didn't respond. A few days later, I came home from work and saw him standing in my backyard. I knew Missy was inside the house, so it really freaked me out seeing him there. I didn't know if he was a peeping Tom or what. I jumped out of my truck and ran as fast as I could toward him. But when I got close to him, I realized he was a really big kid, probably only sixteen years old.

"You might whip me if you decide to fight, but you'll remember this day the rest of your life," I told him.

I proceeded to share the Gospel with him in a very stern voice.

I told him we were hosting a Bible study later that night, invited him to attend, and encouraged him to bring a Bible if he had one. To my surprise, he actually showed up at our house, but instead of bringing a Bible, he brought a bag of marijuana!

"If I'm really going to change my life, I guess I need to get rid of this," he said.

I thought the guy was trying to entrap me with the police, and I was looking in every direction to see if anyone was watching. I invited him into my house and dumped the weed down our garbage disposal. I found out later that the kid's father had left him when he was very young, and his mother wasn't very involved in his life. He'd dropped out of school and wasn't doing much of anything besides smoking weed and drinking beer. He seemed fascinated with gangs and the type of lifestyle that goes along with them. He used a lot of gangster lingo when he spoke, but the scariest part was that his ultimate goal in life was to become incarcerated in the federal prison system. He figured that was the best way he'd be sure to have three meals a day and a roof over his head. The kid attended a few of our Bible studies, and I became a father figure to him. I persuaded him to go back to school and tried to get him to try out for the football team. I'm pretty sure we helped him change his life.

One of the strangest moments in my early days of sharing the Gospel occurred when I was introduced to a guy who suf-

> This guy actually showed up at our house, but instead of bringing a Bible, he brought a bag of marijuana!

fered from Tourette's syndrome. I didn't know him, but I could tell he was starting to get anxious as I read him scripture. He also had a stuttering problem and couldn't put sentences together as he tried to talk to me. All of a sudden, he started shouting four-letter words. I didn't know the guy had Tourette's, so I couldn't figure out what was going on. I feared he might have been demon possessed! The more he blurted out obscenities, the louder I got in sharing the message. It was quite the banter. I was thinking I might have to revisit my thoughts on exorcisms until my buddy told me about his disorder.

Some of the people I met through happenstance became some of my closest friends. One night, Blake and I were driving to share the Gospel with the guy who owned the auto body shop where I'd traded the deer I ran over for a new (but used) radiator. On the way, Blake saw a guy standing next to a sports car on the side of the road.

"Hey, I know that guy," Blake said. "That's Phillip McMillan."

We pulled over and Blake introduced me to Phillip. We invited him to go study the Bible with us.

"Nah, that's not for me," he said.

"Hey, we're going to play cards after," I said. "It'll be a good time."

"I'll go as long as I don't get confronted," he said. "I don't want to be the center of attention."

Well, as soon as we walked into the house, I pulled out my Bible and said to Phillip, "Come over here, son. Let me show you something."

Phillip was very moved when he heard the Gospel. It hit him like a ton of bricks. He was very emotional and asked me to share the message with his girlfriend, Alicia. Missy and I met with her a few days later. Although I could sense Alicia was a religious person, she seemed somewhat offended by what I was telling her. As much as I tried, I couldn't get Alicia to embrace Christ's message.

About a month later, there was a knock at my front door at six o'clock in the morning.

When Missy opened the front door, Alicia was standing there in a driving rainstorm. She had tears in her eyes and was holding a Bible in her hand and told us she had been up all night.

"I can't get around it," she told me.

"Well, what do you want to do?" I asked her.

"Will you baptize me?" she said.

I baptized Alicia, and she and Phillip became two of our closest friends. Although Phillip is very competitive with Willie and me—you might have seen him in our lawn mower race on *Duck Dynasty*—we're actually good friends. They embraced the Lord's message and recommitted themselves to living a pure life.

I believed God sent all these people to me to hear the message of Jesus. Second Corinthians 5:20 says: "We are therefore Christ's ambassadors, as though God were making his appeal through us." In Christianity, how you finish is as important as how you begin. These new friends had been living such hard lives, and I didn't want to lose a single one of them. Many of them came from broken homes and were battling alcohol and drug addictions, and some of them were even involved in prostitution. I felt like it was my responsibility to keep them out of trouble, so I became their mentor and entertainer.

Missy and I hosted three scheduled Bible studies every week. We would always cook and gather around our table for a meal and prayer. We didn't have much money and most of our meals could be found under the title "Forty Ways to Cook a Potato." Everyone considered our home a safe house, so we never locked our doors in case someone showed up in the middle of the night needing a place to stay. There was a men's night, a women's night, and a Sunday-night house church. Sometimes, we had as many as seventy people crammed into our small house, but it never seemed crowded as we prayed together, sang together, and shared how we could become more like Christ. We also hosted movie nights and all-night card games at our house.

Eventually, Missy and I sought the advice of several people to help us balance our marriage and ministries. My parents; her parents; Alan and his wife, Lisa; and our friends Mac and Mary Owen were very helpful and offered us spiritual guidance. They helped us gain a perspective on what was best for us that would still allow us to help others. Any couple will tell you that the first year of marriage is the most difficult because you're still trying to get to know each other. But we were also trying to bring so many people to the Lord in our ministry work.

> We never locked our doors in case someone showed up in the middle of the night needing a place to stay.

No matter what you do in duck hunting, you're not going to get the ducks every time because there are ultimately too many things out of your control. Hey, just because you're sitting in a duck blind doesn't guarantee you're going to shoot a duck! What I finally came to realize about introducing others to Christ is that Missy and I needed to be a team, and we needed to share the message and stop worrying about when, if, or how people responded, even though it was so exciting when they did. There is a spiritual growth process and ultimately everyone has to find their way in their relationship with Christ. Second Corinthians 4:5 says: "We do not preach ourselves, but Jesus Christ as Lord."

There are a lot of ways to encourage people to go to heaven, but you can't carry them there! There was one man in particular who helped me realize that fact. I tried everything in my power to help this guy for years, even jumping into the middle of a fistfight between him and his wife. But no matter how hard I tried, he didn't want to surrender to Christ. I'm just a man; only God can change the heart. Second Corinthians 4:7 says: "We have this treasure in jars of clay to show that this all-surpassing power is from God and not from us."

There are similarities in sharing Jesus and duck hunting, even though Christ offers eternal life to humans and hunting results in death for ducks. They both require teamwork. They also require patience and perseverance. You cannot give up when ducks don't respond to duck calls or people don't embrace the call to Christ. Keep sharing and keep shooting.

Hey, I wish I could produce a guaranteed "rainout" when it comes to bringing people closer to Christ. While I do not want anyone to miss out on possibly living forever with God, I have come to realize that the Christian life is a marathon. People grow in their faith at different paces depending on their own circumstances in life. The key is to share, love, and encourage people to put their faith in Christ, and when they don't respond, we simply offer a place of forgiveness to come back to if or when their heart changes. We do not judge or police those who choose not to accept Christ, but we wish them the best of luck. They're going to need it.

One of my favorite things about the church I meet with is their forgiving spirit for those who go forward every Sunday after the message of Christ is preached and express their desire to change their lives' direction. No one ever responds alone at our church—and a large group of people from the congregation always flocks to the front to join and support them. The response that brings me the most joy is "I'm coming home."

MY BOYS

ESTABLISHING NEW PRIORITIES

Start a child in the way he should go, and when he is old
he will not turn from it.

—PROVERBS 22:6

There are some things in life over which you have absolutely no control. The first such event is your birth. My dad was not present when I was born. He was fishing when my mom went into labor, and she sent Uncle Si to try to persuade Phil to come witness the momentous occasion. His reply was, "What do you want me to do about it?" I guess technically his argument was based on some form of logic. Eventually, he came around and was present when my youngest brother, Jep, was born. Phil described it as a "life-changing event," even though he said at the time that after viewing the birth he believed his future sex life with my mom was officially over. Even though my dad and I have a lot in common, especially when it comes to hunting and fishing, I decided that

> **After viewing Jep's birth, my dad believed his future sex life with my mom was officially over.**

watching each of my own kids being born was something I wasn't going to miss.

I was at the hospital when my older son, Reed, was born on May 15, 1995. As for my younger son, Cole, the circumstances of his birth were similar to what I'd experienced with my dad, but we'll get to that story in a minute. Missy and I decided before our wedding that we weren't going to have any children until after five years of marriage. When you have kids, everything changes, and we wanted to enjoy being together while we were young and lay a spiritual foundation for our family before we had any kids.

The birth of Reed was so excruciating and painful that I wasn't sure Missy would ever want to have another child. She was about ten days past her due date and looked like she was ready to pop at any minute. Missy's doctor asked her to come to the hospital on a Monday morning. The doctor induced her that morning and then didn't show up again until about three thirty P.M. Nothing major was happening yet, so the doctor broke Missy's water and left.

Missy remembers the details of Reed's birth better than I do.

Missy: Soon after the doctor broke my water, I started to feel a more consistent pain, but I did breathing exercises and was able to handle it. However, just a few minutes later, my contractions became much harder, my breathing became very labored, and my stomach started convulsing to where I wasn't able to stay in control. I urged Jase to get the nurse to order the epidural for the pain, which he gladly did. She called the doctor and returned to the room, rolling her eyes at me, which validated my feeling like a wimp. She reported that the doctor said if I was dilated close to four centimeters, I could get the epidural. While the nurse proceeded to check me, I started to pray. I had never prayed so hard for a number in all my life! But then the nurse gasped out loud.

"What is it?" I asked.

"You're at nine centimeters!" the nurse said.

"What does that mean?"

"That means you're going to have to start pushing," the nurse said. "It's too late for an epidural."

Missy started crying and told the nurse she'd paid for the epidural and wanted it right then. Unfortunately, it was too late. Reed was positioned faceup in the womb, instead of facedown, and Missy had to push for two hours without any medicine. Let me tell you one thing: my respect for women grew exponentially that day. Like my dad says, if men were left to do the childbearing, there would be a much smaller population on earth. We'd do it once and that's it! After a couple of hours, the doctors finally gave Missy a local anesthetic and used forceps to pull Reed out. The whole ordeal lasted fourteen grueling hours. When Reed was born, his head was cone shaped because of the forceps. I thought, *Well, he's going to be a little lopsided, but we'll love him anyway.* I didn't know his head would eventually return to a normal shape.

Almost two years later, Missy became pregnant with Cole. Because he was breech, a C-section was scheduled for December 11, 1997, which was right in the middle of the duck season split. That's typically a two-week gap between Thanksgiving and Christmas Day when we can't hunt ducks in Louisiana. I told her it wasn't a great idea to have his birthday then because the first couple of weeks in December are usually right in the middle of the split. During the split, we annually hit the road to hunt ducks in Arkansas, Idaho, Kansas, or somewhere else. It's one of the reasons Cole's birthday is in such a bad spot. I'm usually out of town on his birthday, so we have his party before I leave or after I get back. I told him at an early age, "Sorry, buddy, you came out at a difficult time." But the good news is I usually take him on a hunting trip for his birthday, now that he's older.

Fortunately, the split during the 1997 duck-hunting season occurred a couple of weeks later than it usually does. The day Cole was born, on December 4, 1997, I went duck-hunting with my dad and brothers. During this particular duck season, my dad had noticed an overpopulation of raccoons on his property. I started running traps to manage the problem and make a little extra money. I was getting up at two thirty A.M. to run my traps, and I was catching raccoons, nutria rats, and even a few otters.

> **Let me tell you one thing: my respect for women grew exponentially the day I watched Missy go through labor.**

After checking my traps, I would clean the animals in between shooting volleys in the duck blind. I'd sell both the fur and meat to various customers—nothing went to waste. About ten o'clock that morning, we saw a boat coming toward us. We didn't recognize the boat, so everybody assumed it was a game warden. It was actually a friend of mine, Chad, whom my mom had called to fetch me from the blind. I was in the middle of cleaning a raccoon and had about two-thirds of its hide off. Both of my hands were covered in blood. Hey, if killing raccoons was illegal—and it isn't—I would have been caught in the act! Chad stopped about a hundred yards from us.

"Hey, Jase, your mom called and your wife is having the baby," he said.

My dad interjected, "What do you want us to do about it? You're scaring off the ducks!"

I looked at the raccoon, looked at my hands, and then looked at Chad.

"Okay," I said as I jumped into his pirogue.

Chad paddled me to the riverbank, where my mom was waiting for me.

Meanwhile, Missy was terrified that I wouldn't make it to the hospital in time.

Missy: Cole wasn't supposed to be born until a week later, but I went into labor a few hours after Jase left the house to go hunting. I went to the hospital, where I was placed on monitors. Once my doctors and nurses confirmed I was truly in labor, I started to panic because Jase wasn't anywhere near the hospital.

I was crying because I couldn't get ahold of Kay after I called her the first time, but I eventually reached her. After the problems I had with Reed, I did not want to deliver this baby without Jase. I knew I couldn't do it without him. Well, then the doctors told me they had another C-section scheduled for later that day, and since I was already in labor, they wanted to deliver Cole immediately. I started crying even more after I realized Jason wouldn't be there. I was in pure panic mode! I couldn't believe Jason was going to miss it!

When I reached my truck, I told my mom to let me drive. It usually takes about forty minutes to get from my dad's property to the hospital. Well, I made it in about fifteen minutes! I had my flashers on and when we reached the hospital parking lot, there was smoke coming out from under the hood. I ran into the operating room without even washing my hands. When the doctor saw I was covered in blood, she looked at me like, "What have you been doing?" I told her, "I came from skinning a dead raccoon to watching a live human birth." Amazingly, the doctor never changed facial expressions and told me to wash up.

MY BOYS

Missy: Right after the doctor cut me open, I heard a nurse say, "Guess who's here?" I didn't even know if they were talking to me. I had a sheet in front of me, blocking my view, so I couldn't see anyone. Then they said, "The dad's here." I was like, "I don't want my dad in here!" Once Jason entered the room and I heard his voice, I felt a relief that I can't even describe. He peeked his head around the sheet and said, "Hey, babe," like it was just another ordinary day. He started talking to the doctors and nurses and telling them what all he had been doing that morning, and I heard everyone laughing. I started giggling and laughed the entire time because he was hysterical. I literally went from crying to laughing in a matter of seconds, and he put me at ease emotionally. He told everybody the story about skinning the raccoon while they were trying to get the baby out. After a few minutes, I heard my obstetrician say, "Jason, shhhh, I'm getting close to the baby. She can't laugh anymore, so you're going to have to stop talking."

> They said, "The dad's here." I was like "I don't want my dad in here!"

Cole's birth happened so fast. This is going to sound strange, but when they cut Missy's stomach and popped her open, it seemed eerily similar to what I'd left in the duck blind. Some guys can't handle seeing their wives cut open, but it didn't bother me at all. But when they pulled Cole out, the umbilical cord was wrapped around his neck two full times. I remember thinking, *Uh-oh, my son is in trouble.* For some reason, I lost sense of where I was. It was like I was standing over the hood of a car with a bunch of guys trying to fix something. Well, the doctor was the mechanic and seemed to be having difficulties, so I reached in to help her unwrap the cord from my son's neck. Everybody stopped when I did it, and the doctor looked at me like she was horrified. It was her way of telling me to back away. Thankfully, the doctors removed the cord and Cole was fine.

I was ecstatic to have two sons, and I was determined to be the father my dad was after he became a Christian. I quickly realized that parenting is the most difficult thing to do on this planet. The fact that all kids have different personalities creates a lot of uncertainty in how to handle them. Former heavyweight champion boxer Mike Tyson once said, "Everyone has a plan until they get punched in the face." I think the same thing can be said about parenting: everyone seems to be an expert until they actually have kids.

I decided the best thing I can do as a parent is to spend time with them, love their momma, and introduce them to Jesus. For me, the life I lead in front of them validates the message of Christ, the way I treat Missy is the model they will follow in their interactions with women, and I try to have quality moments with each of my children at least once every day. Whether I'm hunting or fishing with my boys or playing games with them, I always take the time to see where they are in their faith and relationships. One of the things Missy and I started doing when our boys became teenagers was having a big meal with them and their friends every Wednesday before midweek church. It gives us a chance to have spiritual conversations with them and to see who they are running with.

Of course, many of those conversations occur when we are hunting. The first time I took Reed hunting was when he was six years old. I took him on the last day of duck season, and we pulled right up to the water. I gave him a BB gun, and I had my shotgun. Our property was a haven for wood ducks, so that's what I wanted to shoot so he could see what made this spot so special. Wouldn't you know it? The first two ducks that flew in our sights were a mallard drake and hen. We were on a bank instead of in a blind, which was unusual, but the ducks floated down and lit about ten feet in front of us. More than anything, I showed Reed the power of a duck call, because the water in front of us was only about two inches deep. I couldn't believe the ducks were sitting there.

> I decided the best thing I can do as a parent is to spend time with my kids, love their momma, and introduce them to Jesus.

"I'm going to count to three," I whispered to Reed. "Get your BB gun. When I get to three, you fire.

"One, two, three!" I said.

Reed shot his BB gun, and I fired my shotgun at the same time. The drake never knew what hit him, and Reed immediately looked down at his BB gun. It was like he was thinking, *What is this thing?* I don't think he even realized I killed the duck with my shotgun. Reed was so excited that I don't believe he realized that I had shot, despite the fact of the booming sound. He looked back at me, and I told him, "Boy, you put a good shot on him, son."

We brought the duck home, and Missy took a photograph of us with it.

When Reed was old enough to go dove-hunting, I figured out that he was more into shooting shells than actually hunting. He wanted to fire his gun as much as possible. Whenever a dove flew by, I heard boom! Boom! Boom! I tried to tell him that shotguns weren't heat-seeking missiles and that he had to aim at the bird. But when the next dove flew overhead, I heard boom! Boom! Boom! The first time we went dove-hunting, I think he went through two boxes of shells before he finally connected.

Reed was involved in some of our most famous duck hunts; he even has a blind named after him. It's called the Reed Robertson Hole. One year, we were having a really bad duck season. It was hot and there always seemed to be southwest winds, which aren't ideal conditions on Phil's property. One Sunday, the forecast called for more southwest winds, so nobody wanted to go hunting. I wasn't going to pass up a morning in the duck blind, so I decided to take Reed with me. My expectations were so low that I was really only taking him to see the sunrise. I was convinced we wouldn't see a single duck.

Well, it got to be daylight and nothing happened. But we were still spending quality time together, and I was talking to him about God and the outdoors. I looked up and saw two birds. I literally thought it was two crows flying overhead. But then I realized it was two mallard drakes. I called them and they made two passes over our blind before backpedaling right in front of us. They seemed to stop in motion about ten feet in front of us.

"Shoot!" I said.

Reed raised his gun and shot three times in less than three seconds. Apparently, he still believed his shotgun was an AK-47. He went boom! Boom! Boom! By the time Reed was done, I raised my gun and shot both of them. He looked at me and was like, "What happened?" He looked at his gun and thought something was wrong with it.

"Son, you got excited and fired too quickly," I said. "You've got to get on the duck."

As soon as I looked up, I saw ten teals circling toward us. They came right into our decoys. I decided to give Reed the first shot again.

"Cut 'em," I said.

Reed raised his gun and fired again. Boom! Boom! Boom! He shot one and then I shot another one.

"Hey, you're on the board," I said.

A while later, about seventy-five teals made three passes over us. I was going to let them light so Reed could get a good shot. About half of them lit and the other half came right toward us.

"Cut 'em," I said.

I raised my gun and shot two of them. I heard Reed fire three times but didn't see anything on the water.

"I think I got three of them that time," he said.

"Son, don't be making up stories," I told him.

I was looking right where he shot and didn't see anything. But then I looked to the right and realized he'd actually shot four. He hit three on one side and a stray pellet hit one in the back.

"Son, you have arrived," I said.

We wound up killing our limit that day, when I didn't expect us to see any ducks at all. Phil and everybody else made a big deal about it because we hadn't seen many ducks in days. It was the most ducks we'd ever shot out of that blind, and we've never mauled them like that again there. Because I shared the experience with my son, it was one of my most special and memorable hunts. I learned a valuable lesson that day: you never know when the ducks are going to show up. That is why I go every day the season is open.

Much like his birth, Cole's first hunting experience was a little more traumatic. He was five years old and we were getting ready to have our Christmas party at Phil's house in 2002. Because we hunt on private land, we're allowed to shoot deer from our vehicles. Cole and I climbed into my truck right before dark, and I drove next to the woods. As I was explaining safety and other things about hunting to him, a deer walked right into the middle of a trail. We hadn't been there for five minutes before the deer showed up! I looked at Cole and pointed toward the front of the truck.

Without saying anything, I leaned my gun out the driver's-side window of my truck and shot the deer. The deer did a double backflip and hit the ground. I looked at Cole and his mouth was wide open. I could have picked his jaw up from the floorboard.

"That's how you do it, son," I told him.

Cole didn't say anything. I figured his ears were still ringing, and I instantly regretted not telling him to cover them. It ended up being a pretty traumatic experience for him, and I feared he'd never want to go hunting again. In hindsight, he might have been a little too young to witness something like that.

Eventually, Cole came around and wanted to go hunting as much as Reed. I took them hunting for squirrels, deer, and doves. I didn't get to take them duck-hunting as much as I would have liked because we usually film our hunts and it's too dangerous to have kids shooting around cameramen, especially when one of the cameramen is their uncle. I do take them at least a couple of times a year.

Cole's most memorable duck hunt occurred on my dad's property at a blind we call the Lake Blind. We created this great location by cutting down dead trees and cleaning out brush. The blind itself is like a small house; it can hold up to fifteen people. We mauled them that day, and Cole shot a canvasback duck, which is really rare to see in our area. Most of the canvasback ducks in North America are found at the Chesapeake Bay on the

> In hindsight, he might have been a little too young to witness something like that.

East Coast. The duck came in and lit in front of us, and we let Cole shoot it. It gave me the opportunity to explain to him that ducks taste the same whether they're shot flying or sitting. Everybody made such a big deal about it, and he felt like the big man on campus. "Yeah, bring me down here, and I'll get you a canvasback," he said proudly.

Cole killed his first deer when he was about thirteen years old. I was sitting in a deer stand with him, and I saw two deer running toward an opening. They were moving pretty fast.

"When I holler, you shoot," I told him.

As soon as the deer arrived at the opening, I hollered. The deer stopped, and Cole fired his gun. One of the deer hit the ground. Cole looked at me, and then I looked at him. He was grinning from ear to ear. He didn't know blood was pouring down his face. I'd talked to him about shooting a gun and holding it tight. But the gun kicked back and the scope hit him square in the eye.

"You got him," I said. "Oh, my goodness, did you get him! You're going to have a big black eye, too."

"What?" he said as he reached toward his face.

He looked at me like, "What just happened?" I think he actually thought he'd just shot himself.

"Yeah, you're going to have a good scar to commemorate your first deer," I told him. "The first rule is you've got to hold your gun tight when you fire, but it was a good shot."

Kind of like Willie and me, Cole and Reed are polar opposites. Cole is a quiet kid, but when he says something it's usually funny. He takes care of his business and makes good grades. Reed is very talkative and engaging. He manages to pass in school, but he has had to work hard at his studies. However, he is an incredible singer, musician, and artist. He's high-strung and is a live wire but is a natural leader. Cole has a tendency to think things through and analyze them, while Reed tends to be more of a risk taker. Despite their differences, they are two of the finest young men I know and I couldn't be more proud of both of them.

I think the best thing you can do for your kids is to be there for them as much as possible. When my boys were born, I decided

I was going to go to every one of their games if they were involved in sports. It was something I had to grow into because my dad didn't attend any of my sporting events when I was a kid. I can count on one hand the number of times I've missed one of their games. I build my schedule around their baseball and football games. I really enjoy sports and competition and think they're good, clean fun. Sports teach so much about patience, perseverance, teamwork, and life in general. If kids aren't involved in something like sports or hunting and fishing, they start getting into mischief because they're bored.

When my boys were born, I decided I was going to go to every one of their games if they were involved in sports.

When my boys started playing Little League baseball, I was at every game and served as an assistant coach a couple of times. It didn't take me long to realize the problem with Little League baseball wasn't the players but their parents. Some of the things I witnessed coaches and parents do in front of their kids was downright shameful. I spent ten years observing the chaos of Little League baseball before deciding I needed to step in and bring a godly approach to our league. When Cole turned fourteen, I decided to become his head coach in his final season of Little League. I accepted the responsibility like I was the general manager of a Major League Baseball team. I assembled a dream team of coaches: Justin Martin, who works with me at Duck Commander, was my hitting coach; my brother Alan's son-in-law Jay, who was a high school athletics director and coached kids for more than ten years, was my bench coach; and a great friend of mine, Paul Stephens, who coached semiprofessional baseball for twenty years, was my pitching coach. These men knew their baseball, but more important, they were godly men with great character.

I took the job very seriously and called a parents' meeting about every week. I never raised my voice in anger the entire year—nor did any of our coaches—and we always stayed positive. Our top priority was to be godly role models to the boys, and we spent as much time talking with them about their lives as we did baseball. Most of the kids came from broken homes, and some of the boys were incredibly bitter and angry about life. We made the baseball field our "safe place," and I wouldn't allow any outside distractions to enter. We became extremely close and I grew to love every one of those boys as my own. We were one of the least athletically gifted teams in the league, but we finished with a 14–2 record and won the championship. It was my first and last season as a head coach. I figured it couldn't get any better after that.

Both of my sons participate in various sports at Ouachita Christian School in Monroe, which leads to a lot of quality family time for us. Reed played on two OCS football teams that won Louisiana Class A state championships in football in 2011 and 2012, and Cole was on the team as an eighth grader in 2011. When OCS beat West St. John High School 23–7 to win a state title at the Louisiana Superdome in New Orleans in 2011, Missy sang the national anthem before the game and was flanked by our sons. To me it symbolized one of the main reasons they turned out to be such good kids, because they have an incredible mom. It was an awesome moment shared by our family, and the fact that our school won it all made it that much sweeter.

As grand as winning the state championship was, the most gratifying moments in my life were when my two sons surrendered to Christ in baptism. A lot of effort from friends and family helped lead my boys to their decision, and I am filled with gratitude for each and every one of them. I've always been a guy who thinks he can fix everything and figure it out. But then you have kids and you realize, *Hey, I'm going to need some help.* There's really no manual for raising kids. There's no easy way, but God's Word is a good blueprint.

> There are a few people on this earth I would give my life for, and my kids are at the top of the list. However, I am positive that I would not offer my kids' lives for anyone.

In John 3:3, Jesus told a religious man named Nicodemus, "I tell you the truth, no one can see the kingdom of God unless he is born again." Nicodemus thought he was referring to a second physical birth, which would be impossible. Jesus answered in John 3:5: "No one can enter the kingdom of God unless he is born of water and the Spirit." I eventually came to realize that the characteristic I have most in common with my kids is that I am flawed and make mistakes. In Christ we find mutual forgiveness, and our new birth gives us the opportunity to start over with God's spirit in our heart.

There are a few people on this earth I would give my life for, and my kids are at the top of the list. However, I am positive that I would not offer my kids' lives for anyone. I love them too much.

That is the reason my top priority as a parent has been, and always will be, to point them to Jesus. Jesus died on a cross because God gave up His perfect Son in love so everyone on earth could find justice and forgiveness. The fact that Jesus went along with it willingly makes Him worthy of being the ultimate role model for my kids.

10

OUR LITTLE GIRL

DISCOVERING TRUE BEAUTY

*But we also rejoice in our sufferings, because we know
that suffering produces perseverance; perseverance,
character; and character, hope.*

—ROMANS 5:3-4

No one likes pain and suffering, but sometimes bad things happen to us for no apparent reason. One morning on our way to the duck blind, we saw something that was painful to watch. We were in the boat with our normal hunting party and film crew, as my dad was navigating through the backwater on his land. We film every one of our hunts to produce a Duck Commander DVD at the end of every season. On this particular morning, one of our cameramen, Greg, had one of his feet dangling over the bow of the boat. In an instant, Greg was sucked out of the boat, and then we felt the boat run over him. My dad tried to stop, but it was impossible to slow down.

Fortunately, Greg came up on the other side of the boat and quickly jumped back in. It was dark and everyone assumed he had simply fallen out of the boat. There was a brief chuckle and my dad asked, "Greg, you all right?" All he said was, "Nope!" We arrived at the blind and after we shined a flashlight on Greg, we quickly realized he was seriously injured. Somehow, Greg's foot had gotten caught between a stump and the boat, causing him to be ripped from his seat. Greg's leg was badly cut and mangled as the momentum of the boat pulled the rest of his body underwater. Greg was fortunate he wasn't killed, and it took him several months to recover from the accident. The scary incident reminded us how perishable our bodies are.

The earth teems with people who suffer physical afflictions for a variety of reasons. All of us at some point are going to experience pain and suffering, whether from our own actions or happenstance. As parents, it is only natural to try to protect our kids from anything that could potentially cause them pain. By the time Reed was seven and Cole was four in 2002, our lives were free of any major difficulties. Both of our boys were healthy, and they were getting to the age where we didn't have to watch them every second of every day. Slowly but surely, our lives settled into a tranquil routine as Missy and I started to build our family. We loved having two boys, but Missy really wanted a girl. I liked the idea of having a daughter, too, since Miss Kay was the only woman in our house when I was growing up. To be honest, I wasn't sure if Missy could handle being around nothing but men—especially Robertson men—for the rest of her life!

OUR LITTLE GIRL

In the early spring of 2002, Missy was having problems with her birth control medicine. She was suffering from headaches, and I told her to quit taking the pills.

"Let's have another baby," I told her.

"Are you sure we're ready for that?" she said.

"Hey, we can handle it," I said.

Almost a year later, we were excited to learn that Missy was expecting. Unfortunately, due to complications, Missy had a miscarriage. It was a real low point in our lives. A few months later, Missy became pregnant again, and we were cautiously optimistic about our chances for a third child. Her pregnancy had problems from the start. There were concerns about Missy's blood work, and her doctors feared her body might begin to reject the baby. Unless our baby had Rh-negative blood—and her doctors gave us a 1 percent chance of that being the case—Missy would probably suffer a second miscarriage. Doctors told us the goal was for Missy to carry the baby to twenty-six weeks, and then they would remove our child by cesarean section. Missy and I prayed a lot about our baby, and miraculously her blood work gradually improved. (After our daughter was born, doctors confirmed she did indeed have Rh-negative blood. In a lot of ways, she was a one-in-one-hundred miracle.)

Missy and I started to prepare to welcome a third child into our home. We found out at twenty weeks that our baby was a girl, and we decided to name her Mia. I could sense Missy was very excited about having a daughter. She loved our boys, but Missy really wanted to experience the joys of having a daughter too. When Mia was thirty-one weeks along, Missy had a four-dimensional ultrasound, which was fairly new technology at the time. She wanted to see an up-close view of our baby in the womb. Reed, Cole, Miss Kay, and our sisters-in-law Jessica and Lisa accompanied her to the doctor's office to see the baby.

As soon as the ultrasound started, Missy noticed that something was different about Mia's face.

The technician looked more closely at the monitor and then hesitated before saying, "I need to go get the doctor."

Miss Kay took Reed and Cole out of the room, and then the doctor confirmed what the technician feared: our baby had at least a cleft lip. It was too early to determine whether Mia also had issues with her palate, but the doctor warned Missy that there are several potential problems that are typically associated with having cleft lip and palate. My mom called me and told me to come to the doctor's office right away.

> As soon as the ultrasound started, Missy noticed that something was different about Mia's face.

When Missy told me what she'd learned, I said, "Well, we'll just have to teach her that beauty is on the inside."

It wasn't what Missy wanted to hear. As I reflect back on what I said to her, I realize it was actually a dumb thing to say, even though it was true. Proverbs 31:30 says, "Charm is deceptive, and beauty is fleeting; but a woman who fears the Lord is to be praised." Outward beauty is so subjective and is ultimately very temporary. My dad once gave me some advice when considering beauty. He said, "When it comes to women, do not put a lot of stock in outward beauty, because at some point everything heads south." It was a humorous way of saying everyone gets old, but it also reveals the fact that everyone ages and gravity always wins.

Some people spend their entire lives trying to grasp outward beauty, only to chase in vain. I do think it is only natural for potential parents to wish for a perfect-looking child, but to make a big deal of it is foolishness. Romans 9:20 says, "Shall what is formed say to him who formed it, 'Why did you make me like this?'" Since Missy and I believe God knits each human in his or her mother's womb, we were not overly concerned about Mia's outward appearance. Our biggest concerns were about our daughter having to endure multiple procedures and surgeries to correct her health problems. We didn't want our baby suffering in any way, emotionally or physically.

For the next three or four months, we did what most people do when they're faced with adversity. We asked, "Why is this happening to us?" It was three or four months of misery. With each passing day, we became more and more anxious about the birth. But after the initial shock, we began to say, "You know what? We are not going to ask, 'Why us?' We are going to ask, 'Why not us?'" We decided to change our outlook because we knew our baby would need us to be strong. Our trust in God allows us the ability to overcome any obstacles that come our way.

One passage from the Bible that really helped me handle the situation spiritually

> We began to say, "You know what? We are not going to ask, 'Why us?' We are going to ask, 'Why not us?'"

was John 9:1–3, which says, "As he went along, he saw a man blind from birth. His disciples asked him, 'Rabbi, who sinned, this man or his parents, that he was born blind?' 'Neither this man nor his parents sinned,' said Jesus, 'but this happened so that the work of God might be displayed in his life.'" After I thought about that scripture for a while, I thought about my daughter. If she was born alive and found her spiritual relationship with her Maker, in the end we would all win. It took me a while to reach that conclusion because my family is notorious for assessing blame. It's a Robertson trait. But when doctors told us about Mia's condition, I had to quit playing the blame game. I had to say, "We're going to embrace it and manage it." Romans 8:31 says, "If God is for us, who can be against us?"

Fortunately, Missy accepted the situation and ran with it. After we found out about Mia's condition from the ultrasound, we shared our story with our church family the next Sunday and asked them to pray for us. After the service, a couple approached us and told us they had a client whose grandchild was born with a cleft palate. They wanted to have the parents reach out to us for support. The couple told us they'd been working with a craniofacial surgeon in Dallas, Dr. Kenneth Salyer, who had famously separated a pair of conjoined twins from Egypt in 2003. The boys, Mohamed and Ahmed Ibrahim, were given only a 10 percent chance of survival but both made it through their surgeries and are now thriving. Missy e-mailed Dr. Salyer's office, and he agreed to accept Mia as a patient. We viewed it as an answer to our prayers.

When Mia was born on September 12, 2003—she was born about three weeks premature because Missy had high blood pressure—we learned that her palate was also severely affected. She had tissue from the top of her mouth to her nose, but it wasn't fused together. She weighed six pounds, nine ounces, which wasn't abnormally small, but she was suffering from what doctors described as wet lungs. The doctors weren't very familiar with cleft babies, so they rushed her away, believing she couldn't breathe on her own. I heard the doctors and nurses whispering to one another, and then they rushed me out of the room. Boy, I lost it. I went out to tell our family and friends the bad news. I'm not normally an emotional guy, but I couldn't even talk. All I could say was, "I don't know what's going on, but I know it's bad." It was the only time in my life that I was at a loss for words. In my mind I was thinking one thought: *Please, God, let my little girl live.*

Fortunately, Mia only had fluid in her lungs, which is a normal condition with a cleft lip and soft palate, and she was actually breathing on her own. She had to remain in the neonatal intensive care unit until she was able to drink one ounce of formula. It took her six days to pass that threshold, and then we were able to bring her home. The next eleven days were agonizing. It seemed Missy and I spent every minute watching Mia choking, coughing, or gagging with each attempt at taking a normal breath or being fed. We couldn't sleep for more than

> I'm not normally an emotional guy, but I couldn't even talk. All I could say was, "I don't know what's going on, but I know it's bad."

a few minutes without awakening in a panic to check on her condition. When Mia was seventeen days old, Missy and I took her to see Dr. Salyer in Dallas. My mom, Missy's parents, and Missy's aunt Bonny went with us. Her first appointment lasted all day, and it was one of the most grueling experiences of my life. Because Mia was born without a palate, doctors wanted to mold her a temporary one so she could drink and breathe normally until she was old enough and strong enough to have surgery.

I wasn't prepared for what the doctors had to do when they molded a palate for her. They shoved a fistful of material into Mia's mouth. She couldn't breathe, and I bet she had to hold her breath for sixty seconds. The doctors warned us Mia would kick and scream bloody murder, which she did while Missy held her in her lap. It was painful to watch. Then the doctors came back and said the mold didn't work. They were going to have to do it again! I was enraged! I was ready to punch the guy because I didn't think he was being gentle enough with her. Mia was gagging, and I thought she was going to choke to death. I told Missy I couldn't handle watching my baby girl suffer, so I walked out of the room. It was a situation out of my control, and I felt like I was about to hurt somebody. It was then that I realized God was in control of the situation. For some reason, my wife really flourished in this difficult moment. I couldn't deal with it, but Missy was able to handle it. She showed incredible strength and patience, and her motherly instinct took over. She was there to comfort Mia through what had to be excruciating pain and fear.

One thing we quickly learned is that Mia's condition couldn't be fixed but would be managed through multiple surgeries over several years. Mia underwent her first surgery when she was only three months old to repair her outer cleft. She had a second surgery when she was seven and a half months old to correct her palate. She had a third surgery when she was five to do more work on her lip and nose. She's ten now and had her fourth major surgery to graft bone from her hip to her jaw. Because Mia is still growing, the way her bones grow will affect what happens in the future.

I know the surgeries and recoveries are very painful, but Mia has been a trouper and has incredible strength and perseverance. We've actually been blessed because she has undergone the minimum number of surgeries for a child with a cleft lip and soft palate, and she doesn't have any of the other serious medical problems that are sometimes associated with the condition. One thing I've realized through Mia is that kids who go through a lot of suffering have really strong character, and people are drawn to them as a result. As it says in Romans 5:3–4, "Suffering produces perseverance; perseverance, character; and character, hope."

Of course, Mia has lived through some rough days where kids have made fun of her, but it makes for good conversations about good things. Her classmates from Ouachita Christian School have been very accepting of her and don't treat her any differently. She has had to wear headgear twelve to fourteen hours every day. It is designed to help her top jaw align with her bottom jaw. Doctors told Mia she couldn't wear it while she is doing physical activity. Since she sleeps about nine or ten hours every night, she had to wear it for three to five hours during the day. Instead of wearing it while she was home, Mia decided she wanted to wear it to school. She didn't want it cutting into her playtime with her brothers and cousins, when she likes to jump on the trampoline or ride her bike. Mia didn't care what the other kids at school thought about the headgear. When Mia told her doctors in Dallas that she was wearing the headgear at school, they didn't believe her at first. They said they'd never had a child choose to wear it at school. I think it says a lot about her self-confidence and strength.

Our families have been a great support system as we've dealt with Mia's surgeries and health issues. Her cousins adore her and want to be around her as much as possible. Over the years, I've been asked why God allows bad things to happen to good people. I think that's the number one excuse for why some people don't believe in God. But my answer is that God is 100 percent fair. The problem is that some people believe certain things that happen in life aren't fair. It's why I think the Gospel trumps everything else. If God rewards us with forgiveness and eternal life through Jesus, nothing else really matters. If my daughter gets to spend eternity with her family, friends, and God, she'll look back at her life on earth and realize none of her struggles was that big of a deal.

Mia has already persevered through so much. One of our biggest fears when she was born was that she wouldn't be able to talk or sing. My wife loves to sing, and she's a world-class singer. Through speech therapy, Mia talks well and can hold a normal conversation with anyone. There isn't an ounce of shyness in her bones! When Mia was four years old, she sang "God Bless America" on one of our Duckmen hunting DVDs. I'm sure most people who watched it thought, *Hey, isn't that cute? They've got a little girl singing on the DVD.* But when she did it, there wasn't a dry eye in my family. We knew that Mia was born without the ability to sing, and we realized the pain and suffering she endured to be able to sing. It was a huge moment for our family.

I've taken Mia hunting twice and she was like most little girls—she was afraid of the spiders and whatever else was crawling in the blind! The first time, it was only Mia and I, and it was a special day. I gave her a BB gun, and she shot the ducks after I'd already knocked them into the water. I think it took her about fifty BBs before she finally connected, but she had a blast. I didn't know some friends of mine were hunting close by. Later, they told me they heard us shooting and kept hearing a strange sound like a BB gun. They said when she finally connected, they heard us screaming and hollering.

> Mia shot the ducks after I'd already knocked them into the water. It took her about fifty BBs before she finally connected, but she had a blast.

Missy and I haven't spent a lot of time asking God why Mia was born with her difficulties. We have accepted that it's yet another opportunity to glorify Him. A couple of years after Mia was born, one of the nurses at St. Francis Medical Center in

Monroe called Missy. The nurse told her that there was a couple at the hospital, and they had just given birth to a baby with a cleft lip and soft palate. The couple was really struggling with the shock, and the nurse told Missy she remembered how we handled it. Missy and I went to the hospital and talked to the parents. Missy told the nurses to call us whenever a similar situation occurred.

A few months later, Missy and Mia were in Dallas for a checkup. The nurse from St. Francis called Missy and told her there was another baby born with the same condition. Since Missy was out of town, she called me.

"Jason, you have to go up there," she said.

"I can't do this," I said.

"The parents are devastated," she said. "You have to go."

"I can't," I said.

After I hung up the phone, I thought about the situation for several minutes. I remembered how Missy and I felt when Mia was born, and I knew the parents at the hospital needed all the support in the world. I called Missy back and told her I was going. When I walked into the hospital room, the parents were there with some family members. Everybody was crying, and it seemed like the normal joy of a child being born was missing. They looked at me like, "Who is this guy?" It was so quiet I could have heard a pin drop. Their new son was with the other babies in the nursery, and I could see him through the glass wall that separated the waiting room and the nursery.

I'd brought along before-and-after photos of Mia. I took them out of my pocket and held them up.

"I have a girl named Mia, and when she was born she looked a lot like him," I said. "All I can tell you is that you can make it through this. It is going to be okay."

Over the past few years, Missy and I have helped counsel about a dozen families who have children who were born with a cleft lip and palate. We became especially close with four or five families, and a few years ago they came to our house for Christmas. The doctors came to our home from Dallas, and my brother Willie dressed up like Santa Claus. I figured out that God was using us to help others who were dealing with the same things we went through.

> I figured out that God was using us to help others who were dealing with the same things we went through.

I think the Parable of the Workers in the Vineyard in the book of Matthew explains a lot about our journey with Mia. Matthew 20:1–16 says:

For the kingdom of heaven is like a landowner who went out early in the morning to hire men to work in his vineyard. He agreed to pay them a denarius for the day and sent them into his vineyard.

About the third hour he went out and saw others standing in the marketplace doing nothing. He told them, "You also go and work in my vineyard, and I will pay you whatever is right." So they went.

He went out again about the sixth hour and the ninth hour and did the same thing. About the eleventh hour he went out and found still others standing around. He asked them, "Why have you been standing here all day long doing nothing?"

"Because no one has hired us," they answered.

He said to them, "You also go and work in my vineyard."

When evening came, the owner of the vineyard said to his foreman, "Call the workers and pay them their wages, beginning with the last ones hired and going on to the first."

The workers who were hired about the eleventh hour came and each received a denarius. So when those came who were hired first, they expected to receive more. But each one of them also received a denarius. When they received it, they began to grumble against the landowner. "These men who were hired last worked only one hour," they said, "and you have made them equal to us who have borne the burden of the work and the heat of the day."

But he answered one of them, "Friend, I am not being unfair to you. Didn't you agree to work for a denarius? Take your pay and go. I want to give the man who was hired last the same as I gave you. Don't I have the right to do what I want with my own money? Or are you envious because I am generous?"

So the last will be first, and the first will be last.

I doubt you could find anyone on earth who would view the situation in the vineyard as fair. If it happened today, I'm pretty sure there would be lawsuits and perhaps riots in the streets. Life will never seem fair from a human perspective. Jesus told the parable as his disciples were arguing about who was going to heaven. Jesus used the parable to explain that salvation and eternal life come from God alone and are not based on human effort or circumstances. It's a hard truth to embrace, because humans are tempted to take the role of God in declaring fairness. God's rewards and blessings are available to everyone without exception. Second Peter 3:9 says, "The Lord is not slow in keeping his promise, as some understand slowness. He is patient with you, not wanting anyone to perish, but everyone to come to repentance."

God has blessed us with a beautiful daughter who is completely healthy, though she has suffered a lot. Her situation might have been a lot worse, and she's going to lead a productive and full life. The bottom line is, Mia was born with some problems because she was born with a perishable body. We live in a broken world and not until the next world will all be made complete.

But Mia is a flower in the midst of challenges. Her situation has been used by God to form relationships between us and people in similar circumstances. Mia has a great personality, and she's very funny. She lights up the room when she comes into it, and she doesn't get down because she has physical problems. Mia has faced plenty of suffering in her life, but she has persevered, built tremendous character, and given hope to all of us.

Before Mia's first surgery, we were warned that she would look extremely different after the procedure. We were told it's difficult for parents to deal with. Since we were more concerned with her quality of life than how she would look, we didn't think it was a big deal. Boy, were we wrong! When Mia was wheeled out after surgery, Missy and I were shocked. To the doctor and nurses, the surgery was a great success, and they were so excited that there were no complications. We didn't realize that we had accepted all of her differences as part of her makeup and uniqueness. In our eyes, they were part of who she was, and we loved every inch of her. After Mia's third surgery, most people would never even have noticed she had any problems. We are so blessed that she is beautiful on the outside and the inside.

The moments when we had to hand Mia off to her doctors for each of the surgeries were the most painful times of my life. Each time, it was as if someone ripped the soul out of my body. Even though Missy and I knew the surgeries were for the best and Mia's doctors and nurses truly cared about her, it didn't make it any more bearable. When you know your child is about to suffer excruciating pain, your heart aches. We did it because her life was going to be better for it.

> Each time we had to hand Mia off to her doctors for a surgery, it was as if someone ripped the soul out of my body.

I can't help but think of how God, our Father in heaven, handed over His child to people who despised Him, criticized Him, spit on Him, and couldn't wait to kill Him. God knew the intense suffering and prolonged pain His Son would bear, His Son who never did anything wrong. In the ultimate display of love, His Son became the only way we could have a relationship with God. His Son is the reason we can *all* be His children, forever. John 3:16 says, "For God so loved the world that he gave his one and only Son, that whoever believes in him shall not perish but have eternal life." He freely gave His Son over to death for us. He did it because our lives would be better for it.

11

FACIAL PROFILING

JUDGING A BOOK BY ITS COVER

But the Lord said to Samuel, "Do not consider his appearance or his height, for I have rejected him. The Lord does not look at the things man looks at. Man looks at the outward appearance, but the Lord looks at the heart."

—1 SAMUEL 16:7

You know one of the things I dislike most? False advertising. When I was a young kid, I stumbled across an ad in the back of a comic book. Some company was selling magic shrinking dust in a small bottle for only $9.99, plus shipping and handling. The ad featured a life-size cartoon of a young boy with his miniature parents and pets hanging out in the pockets of his shirt and jeans. I remember thinking, *Now that's what I am talking about!* I saved my money for months and mailed thirteen dollars to the address in the magazine. I went out to the mailbox every day in great anticipation of my magic dust arriving. Hey, I also didn't want anyone finding the package before me, because I planned on making a few surprise changes around the Robertson house. Well, the package never arrived. Since I was a kid, I figured there must have been some sort of shipping mishap—until I took a class called physics in school! Then I realized I'd been duped through the power of marketing.

Another pet peeve of mine is receiving a crappy gift that is deceitfully wrapped in fancy packaging. I learned the hard way that when giving a gift to a woman, you should never put anything besides jewelry inside a jewelry box. The sheen and shine of the package can be very deceptive!

People are the same way. When I was in high school I became enamored with a stunningly gorgeous girl. I passed her every day at the same spot during a class change. After doing a little research on her, I rearranged my schedule after midterm to take a class in "home and family" because she was in there. As I entered the classroom, it seemed like destiny—or at least a scene from a sappy chick flick—because my seat was right beside hers! Unfortunately, I quickly ascertained from the first words out of her mouth that she was one of the most vile, obnoxious people I'd ever been around. My attraction immediately vanished, so I looked around the class for other potential candidates. Not only did I not find any girls I might be interested in but I also realized I was the only guy in the class! It was fate gone woefully wrong, but at least the class included a great cooking segment, which I actually enjoyed. Plus, it was an easy A—and there never seemed to be enough of those.

FACIAL PROFILING

Through those two life experiences, I learned a lot about false advertising. The fact that someone wears a nice tailored suit, shaves his face every day, and has a big smile doesn't necessarily mean he's a nice person. Conversely, just because someone has a big beard and long, shaggy hair and wears camouflage doesn't always mean he's a danger to society. Before *Duck Dynasty* came along, you wouldn't have believed some of the looks people gave me while I was walking through an airport or grocery store. People were literally scared of me because of the way I looked.

People talk about racial profiling all the time, and it's hard to argue it doesn't exist in America. For whatever reason, some people make unfair judgments of others based on the color of their skin. It's stupidity, and it's sad that discrimination still occurs in the twenty-first century, but it's something our country is struggling to overcome even today. Well, believe it or not, people will even form an opinion of someone based on whether or not they have facial hair. I call it "facial profiling." If I'm in the grocery store and I walk by a woman who doesn't recognize me, she might clutch her children as I pass her. If I'm at a gas station, people sitting in their cars might lock their doors if they see me coming. It's a subconscious reflex. Some people look at me and immediately think, *There's trouble right there.* And they don't even know me!

I was recently pulled over by the police in the wee hours of the morning on my way to vacation in Alabama. I was traveling with my family, and my wife and kids were asleep. I was on the phone with my brother Al, trying to get directions to our beach house. There was no one else on the road as I was driving through a small town. All of a sudden, flashing lights appeared out of nowhere and I pulled over. The lights woke up everybody in the car, and one of my kids said, "Maybe the policeman watches *Duck Dynasty*." The officer came up to my window and asked for my driver's license and insurance card.

When I began to speak to the policeman, he put his hand on his holstered gun. My wife said, "Guess he's not a fan." The cop gave me a speeding ticket for driving forty-four miles per hour in a thirty-mile-per-hour zone, which was fine. Hey, I broke the law! But what made me a bit uncomfortable was that every time I opened my mouth he put his hand on his gun!

Recently, I was in New York with most of the Robertson family promoting the season-four premiere of *Duck Dynasty*. We were staying at the Trump International Hotel, which is a really nice place near Central Park. I was already uncomfortable being in the big city. I don't like traffic or concrete, and there are a lot of both in New York. After we checked in, we gathered downstairs to go to a Broadway musical show. I know it might seem bizarre for me to be going to a musical, but my very attractive wife can be mightily persuasive, especially when I have nothing else to do.

As we were waiting for the others in the lobby, I asked a doorman if there was a nearby bathroom. He gave me directions to the nearest restroom, which included a walk through the hotel restaurant. As I entered the restaurant, a well-dressed staffer offered his assistance. I informed him I was only going to the restroom. But he very nicely continued to offer assistance and took the role of my escort, which I thought was quite courteous and professional. At his direction, we took a quick left turn and walked out of the hotel. Befuddled, I asked him, "Where is the bathroom?" He pointed down the street or maybe toward Central Park and said, "Good luck to you, sir. Have a nice day." I circled back around to the main entrance of the hotel, where I found Missy, who had witnessed the entire episode.

"I thought you had to go to the bathroom," she said.

I laughed and told her I had been escorted out of the hotel because of the way I looked. It was no big deal to us, and I laughed about the incident later that night with my family over dinner. I shared the story the next day with Kelly Ripa and Michael Strahan on *Live! with Kelly and Michael* because I thought it was funny. Well, the story went viral and was all over the news and Internet the next few days. My phone wouldn't stop ringing and various media outlets were trying to contact me. I'd jokingly labeled the incident "facial profiling" because in my mind that's exactly what it was. People were surprised that it didn't bother me, but my family and I have endured those kinds of things our entire lives. I figured the hotel employee was only trying to protect other hotel guests. The incident culminated with a call from Donald Trump's office. They offered an apology for any inconvenience. I assured them that no apology was needed, and I asked them not to punish my courteous escort.

Some incidents of facial profiling have been more inconvenient than others. I'll never forget walking through airport security when I was flying to give a speech to a Christian men's group in Montana. The Department of Homeland Security screeners obviously didn't recognize me as "Jase the Duckman" from *Duck Dynasty*, and I felt like I was one wrong answer away from being led to an interrogation room in a pair of handcuffs! Hunting season had recently ended, so my hair and beard were in full bloom! The security screeners saw a Bible in my bag, and I guess they figured I was a Christian nut because of my long hair and bushy beard. Somehow, I made it through the metal detector and an additional pat-down, and I guess they couldn't find a justifiable reason to detain me. But as I was getting my belongings back together, I accidentally bumped into a woman. She screamed! It must have been an involuntary reflex. It was a natural response, because she thought I was going to attack her.

Once she finally settled down, I made my way to the gate and sat down to compose myself. After a few minutes, a young boy walked up and asked me for my autograph. *Finally*, I thought to myself. *Somebody recognizes me from* Duck Dynasty. *Not everyone here believes I'm the Unabomber!* Man, I could have used the kid about twenty minutes earlier, when I was trying to get through security! I looked over at the boy's mother, and she was smiling from ear to ear. I realized they were very big fans. I signed my name on a piece of paper and handed it to the kid.

"Can I ask you a question?" he said.

"Sure, buddy," I said. "Ask me anything you want."

"How much does Geico pay y'all?" he asked.

My jaw dropped as I looked at the kid.

"Wait a minute, man," I said. "I'm not a caveman!"

"What do you mean?" the boy asked.

"I'm Jase the Duckman," I said. "You know—from *Duck Dynasty*? Quack, quack?"

It didn't take me long to realize the boy had no idea what I was talking about. In a matter of minutes, I went from being a potential terrorist to being a caveman selling insurance.

I guess it might have been worse. A couple of summers ago, my brother Willie and I went to New York on a business trip. He was going to meet with executives from A&E about our TV show, and I was going to give a duck-calling seminar to a group of hunters in New Jersey. As luck would have it, the New York Yankees were playing the Kansas City Royals at Yankee Stadium, so we decided to attend a game to see our friend John Buck, who was catching for the Royals.

On the morning of the game, we were standing outside our hotel in Manhattan, drinking three-dollar cups of coffee as we waited for a taxi to take us to the A&E headquarters. Some guy walked by us and dropped a few coins in Willie's cup. He thought Willie was a homeless man! Obviously, Willie was stunned, and mad that he had to buy another cup of coffee, but I thought it was hilarious! Here we were standing in New York, meeting with television executives about a reality TV show based on our family and hanging out with Major League Baseball players, but some guy thought Willie needed a few bucks! I actually took a lot of happiness from the fact that the guy thought Willie looked more pathetic than me! The bottom line: when people see our beards, they figure we're either homeless or dangerous.

Here's one thing you have to understand about our beards: We're not growing them; they're growing on their own! Since Phil's beard is so long, people often ask him how long he's been growing it. His response is always the same: "I'm not growing it. It grows by itself." When I was young, Phil liked to compare shaving to mowing the grass, both of which he views as a complete waste of time. One day someone asked him, "Phil, you know, your grass is four feet high. You ever thought about mowing it?" I wondered what Phil's answer would be because I was a little embarrassed about our yard myself.

> I actually took a lot of happiness from the fact that the guy thought Willie looked more pathetic than me!

When the school bus driver dropped my brothers and me off at our house, people liked to ridicule us about how tall the grass was. You could have gotten lost in our yard! But Phil said, "Nah, the frost will get it." In the end my dad's prediction came true; the frost did get the grass, every winter.

Researchers have determined that the average man will spend thirty-three hundred hours shaving during his lifetime. Folks, that's almost five months of your life, which is equivalent to two whole duck seasons! There are up to twenty-five thousand whiskers on the average man's face, and it takes him up to six hundred strokes to scrape his entire face. Surely we can come up with something more productive to do with our time!

Phil likes to tell my brothers and me that men only shave because the advertising executives at Schick and Gillette have convinced the world that men have to shave their faces to be civilized. Phil claims they've fooled the world and become millionaires by doing it! Well, guess what? American men spend an estimated $2.4 billion annually on razors and shaving cream. Have you seen the price of razors nowadays? You have to spend fifteen bucks to get a piece of molded plastic and a cartridge of three or four razor blades! Then they trick you into spending twenty bucks on a pack of replacement cartridges! Remember: a beard grown is a lot of pennies saved.

Of course, the Robertson beard tradition started with my dad. I think Phil started growing a beard because he was self-employed and enjoyed the pleasure of not having to shave every morning before going to work. When he was commercial-fishing on the Ouachita River across from our home in West Monroe, Louisiana, and then making duck calls in the early days of Duck Commander, he didn't have a boss. He was never very good at following orders (maybe that is where I got that from). Because Phil's formative years occurred during the hippie movement of the 1960s, he was kind of antiestablishment anyway. After Phil left teaching to become a fisherman and hunter, he thought, *I'm going to do what I want. There ain't no dress code out here, and there aren't any rules as far as grooming.*

I think the last time Phil shaved his beard was in 1988. He lost a gentlemen's bet to a preacher, shaved his beard, and wore a suit to church, which caused mass chaos among the congregation. Phil said he would never do it again. The bet was over predicting how many people would attend a church service put on by our family and a few friends in an African-American neighborhood. We had a huge fish fry, followed by singing and sharing the Gospel. My dad didn't think many people would show up because we were white and bearded. But they showed up by the hundreds, and some of the people accepted Christ and became good friends of ours that we have to this day. It was a good lesson for everyone that God's message to humanity is colorblind. The Son of God brings all men together like nothing else on earth.

If Phil is anything, he's comfortable in his own skin, and he made sure to pass on that self-confidence to his sons. So that's where the Robertson men's famous beards came from. We don't care what other people think about our hair or beards. We realize not everyone is blessed with the ability to grow a full, masculine beard, but we're not going to judge someone for having less facial hair. There is a place in our society for people with smooth faces; it's called the ladies' room. That's a redneck joke. When I was younger, my dad would tell us, "Number one, you're wasting time if you shave. Number two, God made you have hair on your face for a reason." Phil even quoted Shakespeare when preaching to us about the virtues of having a beard: "He that hath a beard is more than a youth, and he that hath no beard is less than a man."

Phil also used to say, "God made women to have smooth faces." But then he spoke at a conference in Arkansas. From that day forward, he amended his speech to say, "God made *most* women to have smooth faces." That's a Louisiana joke, folks, and

> Phil used to say, "God made women to have smooth faces." But then he spoke at a conference in Arkansas.

my apologies to beard-sporting women everywhere. Like Phil says, "Whiskers on a woman, it's a bummer." But I would add, "It is not necessarily a deal breaker."

Since we're duck hunters, our beards come in handy. Whiskers are really the greatest things you can have in a duck blind during Louisiana winters. The skin tightens up when it's cold. When you're boating down the river before daylight—running forty miles per hour when it's thirty degrees outside—if you don't have a beard, you're out of luck. Whiskers keep your neck warm and prevent your lips from getting chapped. And then, of course, a beard is great camouflage, which is so important in duck hunting. If you have enough gray hair in your beard, it might even look like moss hanging from a tree! All of our beards are different. One of the questions I get asked most often about our beards is why Uncle Si's is shorter on one side. Well, here's the answer: If your beard is caught between your shoulder and your shotgun when you fire, it's going to be pretty painful. The whiplash will literally rip the whiskers out of your beard, and that's why Si's is shorter on the right side!

One thing I've learned over the years is that while I might stand out in public because of the way I look, it's exactly the opposite in the hunting world. A lot of the guests we take duck-hunting show up clean-shaven. They look completely out of place. I mean, they almost look like freaks in the blind because everything else (and everyone else) is rough and dirty. Of course, left alone they wouldn't shoot as many ducks as we do, because their faces look like a full moon and the sun reflects off their mugs like a tin roof.

That's the easiest way to spook ducks. By the end of the hunt, our guests are almost embarrassed about the way they look, which they should be. To me, if you shave, you're not using the resources that God gave you as a provider. You're just not using your head.

Now, I was a bit of a late bloomer when it came to growing a beard. Heck, I was a late bloomer when it came to growing. If you looked at pictures of me in a yearbook from elementary or middle school, you probably wouldn't think it was me because I was so short. But then between my junior and senior years of high school, I grew from five feet tall to six one. My facial hair quickly followed.

I shaved most days before school, but I wouldn't shave during the holidays, when it was also duck-hunting season. After I married my wife, Missy, I only kept my beard during hunting season. Hunting was kind of a crisis for her during the early days of our marriage because I was gone every day for about three months straight. So I let my beard grow throughout hunting season, and then on the last day of the season, I would shave my beard completely off. It was kind of a peace offering to Missy for enduring the previous three months.

For whatever reason, Missy is the only Robertson wife who doesn't like beards. Willie's wife, Korie; Jep's wife, Jessica; and Alan's wife, Lisa, all love my brothers' beards, and I'm pretty sure my mom, Kay, couldn't imagine Phil without a beard because he has worn one for so long. But Missy is consistent in her distaste for facial hair. I hoped that one day my beard would, ahem, grow on her, but it hasn't. Missy once tried to get me to shave by threatening not to shave her legs or under her arms. It actually worked once, but the next time I decided to call her bluff and, well, she was bluffing.

My tradition of shaving on the final day of hunting season lasted until *Duck Dynasty* started. Now I keep the beard year-round because we're filming episodes all the time. The last time I completely shaved my face, my daughter, Mia, was about five years old. I had to go to the barbershop to get my beard shaved off because it was so thick and long. When I walked in, the look on the barber's face was priceless. We both knew I was fixing to get my money's worth. When I came home, I walked in the door and Mia started crying. She even took off running! She didn't know who I was! She wouldn't speak to me for about a week out of fear. Finally, she realized it really was me. That was the last time my face was ever completely smooth.

Like most things in my life, there's also a spiritual side to my beard. Look at John the Baptist, one of the most important people in the New Testament. According to Matthew 3:4, "John's clothes were made of camel's hair, and he had a leather belt around his waist. His food was locusts and wild honey." He baptized Jesus, who was God in human body, despite his appearance being that of a deranged vagrant. When I try to visualize John the Baptist, I see a bearded hunter who had to have some sort of weaponry to function in the wild. I would also assume he dipped the locusts in wild honey before he ate them. Based on what I read in the Bible about John the Baptist, I actually tried to eat a locust once, but it tasted terrible, which gave me the idea that John the Baptist probably dipped them in honey first. Then again, almost everything tastes good with honey.

What I realized is that God used a bearded, animal-skin-wearing, locust-eating wild man to prepare the way for His Son's ministry to the people of the earth. But John the Baptist didn't look religious in any way. God told Samuel in 1 Samuel 16:7, "Man looks at the outward appearance, but the Lord looks at the heart." It is the heart of a man that counts; the beard, in my opinion, is the exclamation point. If you believe a man's heart is right and his spiritual qualities are good, why would you judge him based on how much he shaves his face? As it says in Matthew 7:15, "Watch out for false prophets. They come to you in sheep's clothing, but inwardly they are ferocious wolves." After I thought about that, I decided I would rather be a sheep in wolves' clothing than vice versa, you know?

I think the fact my brothers and I look so different from everyone else has helped us learn to accept others for who they are. Phil and Kay have always believed that judging a person by his or her outward appearance is ridiculous. In other words, they taught my brothers and me that you shouldn't judge a book by its cover. We were taught that, regardless of a person's skin color, clothes, or facial hair, God made every one of us from the same stuff. Acts 17:26–27 says: "From one man he made every nation of men, that they should inhabit the whole earth; and he determined the times set for them and the exact places where they should live.

> It is the heart of a man that counts; the beard, in my opinion, is the exclamation point.

God did this so that men would . . . find him." If God made the first man from dust and the first woman from a rib, it's not hard for me to believe He could individually knit us together in our mother's womb. We are made on purpose, for a purpose, and that makes each individual a masterpiece created by an almighty God.

Everyone is made in the image of God, which means that we are not junk, mistakes, or accidents. This also causes us to realize that life is a gift. We did not choose our existence, and there is no one on earth who is exactly like any one of us. Therefore, I won't judge another person by his or her external appearance. Over the years, I've learned that there is a lot more to having a meaningful life than outward appearance, how much money you have, or whether you're famous or not. I'm not into those materialistic things. It's nice having the blessings of a successful business and popular TV show, but that's never been our motivation in doing what we've done. In my opinion, fame is not about being recognized; it's about recognizing that the God who made you makes us all famous.

Here's the last thing you need to know about my beard: if my life ever gets too chaotic from the popularity of *Duck Dynasty*, my beard will be the first thing to go. In the back of my mind, I have comfort knowing that if I ever become too recognizable, I only have to shave my beard to become anonymous. Not many people outside of West Monroe, Louisiana, would know me without a beard. I think there are a few photos of me without a beard floating around the Internet, but I'm confident I'd be largely unrecognizable with a smooth face. It might sound kind of ironic, because a lot of people grow a beard or wear a fake one for a disguise, but I'm the exact opposite. Shaving is my exit strategy, and it might end up being what ultimately keeps me sane.

With or without a beard, I know I'll be the same guy. I learned a long time ago that it's what's in my heart that matters most.

12

---·◆·---

CAMOUFLAGE

BECOMING ONE WITH THE HABITAT

They exchanged the truth of God for a lie, and
worshiped and served created things rather than the
Creator—who is forever praised. Amen.

—ROMANS 1:25

John 3:16 is the most quoted and recognized passage of scripture from the Bible in the world, and rightfully so. That was the first verse I was able to quote from memory, and it is a great summary of the whole Bible. The Robertson family became enamored with another passage of scripture in the Bible, and it is found in Genesis 9:2–3. As hunters who live off the land, my family and I have not only repeatedly discussed these words from God but we also cherish the verses to this day.

Basically, God declared to Noah and his family that there would be five food groups on earth—everything that *walks, flies, crawls, swims, or grows.* Up until the time of the great flood, people ate only things that grew from the ground. But after the flood, God said, "The fear and dread of you will fall upon all the beasts of the earth, and all the birds of the air, upon every creature that moves along the ground, and upon all the fish of the sea; they are given into your hands. Everything that lives and moves will be food for you. Just as I gave you the green plants, I now give you everything." This scripture is the birthplace of hunting, and it forever changed the menu of mankind for the better.

In Genesis 9:2–3, God sanctioned the pursuit of animals for food, and those verses are a centerpiece of many of the speeches I have given over the years. Before God spoke to Noah, animals were evidently not considered wild and existed in total harmony with humans. He put fear and dread into animals toward humans, and the chase began. If God hadn't permitted us to pursue animals, humans would have been left to eat broccoli, celery, and the dreaded "mallow dogs"—a row of marshmallows in a hot dog bun, which makes a poor substitute for the real thing—instead of enjoying gumbo and shish kebabs. A by-product of the new regimen was the need for camouflage.

> God put fear and dread into animals toward humans, and the chase began.

I have always had a passion for the outdoors and especially things that fly. Part of being successful in life is figuring out what you're good at. My hunting and fishing abilities are God-given talents, and I view them as a blessing. My choice of livelihood was not an accident. The love I have for making duck calls and hunting has never been about making money and is certainly not an act for television. They're my passion and they give me great joy. I don't consider myself an expert by any means, but I have always felt more comfortable in the woods than any other place on the planet.

Over the years, I've figured out that two of the biggest mistakes duck hunters make are choosing a poor position for their duck blinds and not properly camouflaging themselves from the ducks. It seems like every duck season, I'll get at least one call at Duck Commander from a hunter somewhere in the world. The guy usually tells me, "Hey, I love your duck calls. They grab the ducks' attention like nothing else, but they will not finish in my decoys. For some reason, the ducks always land two hundred yards from my blind. Do I need another type of duck call?"

"Hey, save your money," I tell him. "You need to move your duck blind two hundred yards to the other side of the lake! It's not about the duck call. You're in the wrong spot, buddy."

My boss and brother, Willie, is not fond of my advice because it doesn't promote the sale of duck calls. I remember being reprimanded by him at a trade show about another response I gave to a potential customer. The guy asked me what the difference was between a forty-dollar duck call and one that cost one hundred and forty. My response was, "About a hundred dollars." Obviously, Willie didn't like my answer, even if I was only trying to be honest.

Look, duck calls are very important in duck hunting. There's a reason Duck Commander sells tens of thousands of them every year. If you don't blow on a duck call, the ducks tend to shy away from decoys because it's not natural for live ducks to sit in silence. We work really hard to ensure that every one of our duck calls sounds exactly like an actual duck. However, scouting the best spot and being camouflaged are way more important to being a successful duck hunter. Uncle Si is one of the few people I know who believes there is a magic sound that hypnotizes, mesmerizes, and paralyzes a duck—no matter where you are or how exposed you are. He believes you can control a duck's mind with the right sound. But what Uncle Si doesn't understand is that every day is different in the duck blind, depending on the weather, food source, and migration pattern. In the grand scheme of duck hunting, there are a lot of things that are more important than duck calls. People think duck calls have way too much power. (Now Willie is really going to be angry with me!)

I don't have any duck calls that I view as special or my favorites, because one of the keys to being a successful hunter is being able to try new approaches when your original plan is not working. The most vital aspect of duck calling is matching the type of call to the species you're calling. Most people use mallard hen calls for all species of ducks, which is not very smart. Of course, if you match the right call with the right species, you also

> Uncle Si believes there is a magic sound that hypnotizes, mesmerizes, and paralyzes a duck.

have to match the decoys to the sounds you're making to have maximum success. I'll spend all summer building various duck calls and then as soon as the season opens, I'll break open a couple of packages and put new calls on my lanyard. I pick the duck calls that match the species that I have seen in our area. I feel like if I'm not building duck calls that I would use, then why am I building them?

What I've learned after nearly four decades in the woods and swamps is that if you don't camouflage your face, body, and gun, you're never going to get ducks in close to you. Wild animals are going to fly away or take off running as soon as they see you. I guess God wasn't kidding way back there in Genesis! The more you're around ducks and study their movements and sounds, the more you understand their behavior. After a while, you begin to act and sound like the ducks, and then they'll fly right to you. If you sound like them and move like them, you won't stand out like a human. Hey, it's one of the reasons we don't shower very much during hunting season. If you smell like Irish Spring soap and Suave shampoo, your scent is going to stick out like a skunk in the woods. But if you smell and look like the swamp and woods, the animals won't view you as a threat even if they see you.

I have been asked a lot of crazy questions about ducks through the years. Here are a few of them:

1. *Does a mallard hen's quack echo?* No! In spite of assertions that the apparent lack of echo from a mallard hen

is an auditory illusion, I contend that God created the mallard sound so that it doesn't echo—all this for the long-term protection against predators, and maybe to make scientists scratch their heads. I actually invented a call named "Brown Sugar" that doesn't echo. Scientific evidence has proved that some ducks' quacks do indeed echo, but not the mallard hen's.

2. *How many feathers does a typical adult mallard have?* Around ten thousand. They make comfy pillows.

3. *Do ducks cross-breed with other species of ducks?* Yes, although it's rare. If they cross-breed, their offspring are dubbed "mule ducks," and they cannot reproduce. I have personally shot a mule duck that was a cross between a pintail and a mallard. I have seen many other combinations. Another interesting and noble fact about ducks is that they're monogamous during breeding season!

4. *Can ducks smell humans?* In my opinion, yes!

Most of my conclusions are based on my own experiences in the duck blind. We took a hunting trip in West Texas, and the first morning we had ducks pouring into our duck hole. We had ducks come into our decoys and just sit there while we tried to get bigger bunches to join them. During the hunt, we noted that not a single duck got up from the water until we started shooting at them. When we went back the next day, the exact opposite happened. The ducks wouldn't sit in the decoys but a few seconds before they got up without incident and flew away. After a lengthy discussion, we deduced the only change from the previous day was the direction the wind was blowing. The day the ducks sat in our decoys, the wind was blowing in our face from where the ducks were sitting. The second day, the wind was at our backs blowing right toward the ducks. We concluded that the ducks sensed our presence because of our odor.

I've become so adept at concealing myself in the woods that my buddies dubbed me the "Stilker" several years ago. The term was meant to be a combination of "stalker" and "slipper" in the wild. I've learned to adapt to being in the wild and bring back a lot of game by simply "stilking" through the woods. I can walk within a few feet of deer and turkeys because I don't stand out like a human in the woods. Animals are curious, especially if they don't know what you are. When I go slipping through the woods, I notice more animals when I look for things that are out of place, instead of the animals themselves.

One day Mike Williams and I were in the woods cutting firewood, and I saw what I believed was a squirrel's ear protruding above some limbs in the fork of a tree. Mike thought I was mistaken, and we began to argue about it. As most redneck arguments go, it resulted in a friendly wager. I grabbed my gun out of the truck and shot through the branch where I thought the rest of the squirrel was sitting. The branch I shot through fell to the ground, and Mike immediately demanded payment and began cackling and ridiculing me. A few seconds later, we heard more limbs breaking and the dead squirrel crashed to the ground.

Camouflaging yourself is probably the most important part of duck hunting. Sometimes, we're so concealed that we're in danger! Several years ago, during the season split in Louisiana, we went duck-hunting on the Platte River in Nebraska. We were there for three days and shot a few mallards each day. The scenic beauty of the place made up for the small quantity of ducks we shot. Like a lot of other road trips, we went up and down the river, looking for signs of ducks. Once we found a spot, we moved in before daylight, built a temporary blind, and put out our decoy spread. Then we positioned our cameramen to best capture the action and concealed them as much as possible. On the last day of our trip, we set up on a high bluff on the river, which made it feel like we were hunting out of a blind in a twenty-foot-tall tree. We shot a few ducks early in the morning, but then the action really slowed down. We were blowing our duck calls every few minutes, but we were pretty quiet as we waited for the midmorning mallards to make their move.

Suddenly, I caught a glimpse of something moving behind me. When I turned, I saw two coyotes standing in an ambush position. They were watching my brother Jep, who was working as our cameraman and was positioned to the right of us. The coyotes saw Jep moving, but because he was so camouflaged, they apparently didn't realize he was a human. Our guide in Nebraska had warned us that he'd seen several coyotes jump from the top of the bluffs to the ducks below for a quick meal. The landowner was having a lot of problems with the coyotes, which were suspected of killing some of his farm animals. He even feared a few of them might have rabies. Evidently, the coyotes heard us blowing our duck calls and believed we were actual ducks. Now they were ready for their next meal. We had accidentally called in two predators using our duck calls and in essence became the hunted instead of the hunters!

The two coyotes were licking their chops and were about to attack the only unarmed member of our hunting party! It was like a scene out of a bad horror film called *Killer Coyotes*. I looked at Jep and realized he was oblivious to what was going on behind him. I jumped out of our makeshift blind and ran toward the coyotes. One of the coyotes took off running, but the other one ran about twenty feet and stopped. It turned around and started growling at me. It looked at me like,

> We had accidentally called in two predators and had become the hunted instead of the hunters!

"Hey, you want some of me?" I raised my shotgun and shot it dead. I had planned on shooting only ducks, but it's a bad move when a coyote decides it wants to fight a human. Once it stood its ground and said, "You or me," I wasn't going to take a threat from a wild scavenger.

It was a prime example of what happens when animals become overpopulated and lose their fear of humans. The lesson learned: don't bring claws and teeth to a gunfight.

I will always view humans as being superior to the animal kingdom and will continue to manage their habitat and population until I see animals pick up a weapon. It is a dangerous thing to view an animal as having greater worth than a human or even God. It's troubling to see people deny the existence of God and elevate the importance of animals above humans. Romans 1:21–23 says: "For although they knew God, they neither glorified him as God nor gave thanks to him, but their thinking became futile and their foolish hearts were darkened. Although they claimed to be wise, they became fools and exchanged the glory of the immortal God for images made to look like mortal man and birds and animals and reptiles." This type of thinking leads to immorality and impurity in the face of God. Romans 1:25 says: "They exchanged the truth of God for a lie, and worshiped and served created things rather than the Creator—who is forever praised. Amen."

We have a list of priorities in the Robertson household: God, people, and ducks—in that order. We trust God's order of things, and while we love animals, we value human life as the most sacred on earth.

Scouting is another important part of duck hunting. You have to understand the fly zones and patterns of ducks and what species of ducks are migrating in your area. You look for discoloration in the water and feathers to see if ducks have been on your property. Whenever you see one feather, that usually means there were ten ducks there. If there's food around, you look to see how much of it has been eaten. You can get a pretty good idea of how many ducks were there without even seeing one. We'll usually go to the blinds at night, and we'll use spotlights to walk through the water to see if there's been any disruption in the vegetation. If we see signs of movement and feathers, that's where we'll hunt come daylight. Since deer season falls in the middle of duck season in Louisiana, I usually carry a rifle with me while I'm scouting, in case I see a buck. Even when I do see one, I don't usually shoot it because I don't want to disturb the ducks. It has to be a big buck—or a tasty-looking doe—if I'm going to shoot.

Shortly after we returned from the Platte River in Nebraska, I scouted a few of our duck holes on my dad's property. I wanted to see what kind of ducks had gathered on our land while we were gone. On this particular day, it was cool and crisp as it got close to sunset. As I sat in a deer stand waiting for nightfall, I was counting mallards that flew over my head. Meanwhile, there were fox squirrels scurrying in the trees around me look-ing for acorns, while groups of wood ducks waited in the water for the squirrels to drop acorns. A few minutes later, fifteen wild turkeys walked in front of me. I thought to myself, *Man, this is paradise.* As I soaked in my surroundings, I heard the sounds of footsteps in shallow water. A majestic eight-point buck walked right in front of me. I raised my rifle and fired. The buck hit the ground. My dad was in the woods with me and heard me shoot. As we loaded up the deer, I shared the details of what I had seen with my dad. We both agreed that there is nothing better than the beauty of the outdoors. It was about as perfect a day as I've ever had in the woods.

Other days in the duck blind haven't been as perfect. Over the years, we've hunted in all types of weather conditions. We've hunted in hurricanes, rainstorms, and, well, poop storms (we'll get to that in a minute). Regardless of the weather or circumstances, I'm rarely going to skip a day in the blind during duck season. I can only remember one day when I didn't get out of bed to go hunting with my dad—and that was when I was a kid. When my dad tried to wake me, I rolled back over and told him I didn't want to go. As I lay in my bed over the next couple of hours, I heard the volleys as they were shooting ducks. I felt sick to my stomach each time I heard the guns fire. I vowed I'd never skip a hunt again, and I haven't unless I was out of town or severely ill.

About the time Phil set out to film the first *Duckmen of Louisiana* video in 1987, there had been a really bad ice storm in West Monroe, which was kind of rare. It was so cold that a lot of the water on our property froze, so there was nowhere for the ducks to go. We climbed into our trucks and headed south to find the ducks. When we arrived at Lake Maurepas in South Louisiana, our guide took us to a hunting camp that was located about eight miles into the swamp. As we made our way to the camp near sunset, there were so many ducks flying overhead that duck feces started hitting the boat like it was a hailstorm—that's what we call a poop storm! The sound of all those ducks was like a roar. The ice storm had pushed all the ducks south. It was the most ducks I'd ever seen.

The next morning, we called in a group of about three thousand ducks! They funneled into our decoys like a cyclone. It took them over thirty minutes to land. Hundreds of ducks landed in front of us and swam to the edge of our hole, and then more would land in the vacated areas. We sat in stunned silence during the entire event. Finally, Phil whispered to us to

> There were so many ducks flying overhead that duck feces started hitting the boat like it was a hailstorm—that's what we call a poop storm!

be careful because we might kill more ducks than we needed with stray shot, since there were so many of them and they were so close together. My dad thought he saw a rare duck and without warning broke the silence with a gun blast. The roar of the ducks getting up was deafening. We only shot once per hunter and had our limit. It would have never happened if we hadn't been completely concealed in our blind. It was one of the most amazing sights I've ever seen.

At the start of teal season in September 2008, Hurricane Gustav was churning off the coast of Louisiana. It was a category 2 storm and caused billions of dollars in damage in Cuba, Haiti, Jamaica, and the Cayman Islands. When the storm made landfall near Cocodrie, Louisiana, on September 1, it drove most of the teal population north—right back into our flyway. We realized there were going to be a lot of teals on our property, and we weren't going to miss the chance to shoot them—even if driving rainstorms and high winds were coming with them!

The day before Hurricane Gustav was supposed to arrive in West Monroe, I drove to my parents' house so I wouldn't get stranded in town. The next morning, we had a difficult time getting to the blind because there were so many trees and power lines lying over the roads. We eventually made it to the blind, where it was raining sideways because of eighty-mile-per-hour winds! We ran out of shells because the wind was blowing our shot off course! Even though those were miserable conditions, it was one of the most memorable hunts of my life.

Fortunately, I didn't have to chase down a wounded duck that day. What a lot of people don't understand about hunting is that if you shoot and hit a duck but don't kill it, you're legally obligated to make an attempt at retrieving it. Over the years, I've become a better retriever than our dogs. It's an entirely different set of circumstances when you're tracking a wounded duck. I look for feathers, bubbles or ripples on the water, or anything else that looks out of place. You don't actually look for the duck; you look for a trail and signs of where it's headed. I get into "Stilker" mode and chase the trail, and it usually leads me to the duck. I would estimate that if I go after a downed bird, I bring it back 99 percent of the time. I have a treasure chest full of memories in which someone lost a bet with me on whether I would return with a downed duck. These days I have to give very favorable odds to make a bet happen.

Phil has always said I'm better than a dog at retrieving wounded ducks. During one hunt, Uncle Si shot a mallard drake, and it took off charging after it was hit. The duck went flapping across the water and was out of sight in a matter of seconds. The most important aspect of duck retrieval is speed. I jumped from the blind and was running wide open in hot pursuit, and our dog was swimming behind me. I must have followed the duck for more than a mile. I was running in my waders, which were getting wet as I kept falling into the water while jumping over stumps and trees.

> Phil has always said I'm better than a dog at retrieving wounded ducks.

After about a mile, I heard the dog yelp behind me. I didn't know if it had been bitten by a snake or hurt itself on a jagged limb. The dog actually suffered a heart attack because it was swimming so hard. I was going as hard as I could go, the dog was going as hard as it could go, and the duck was going as hard as it could go. A couple of guys from the blind rescued the dog, and I kept going and found the mallard drake. I found it hiding in a brush pile on the bank. It took me a couple of days to recover from that retrieval, and unfortunately, it cost me a dog. The dog survived, but its hunting career was over. Retrieving is one of the reasons why I shoot a tight choke. I don't like crippling ducks; I want to either kill them or miss them. But every once in a while, you'll clip one, and the chase is on.

One of the reasons concealment is so important is because animals live in the woods and humans only visit the wild. Animals make their homes throughout the woods. Just like I'm alert to someone pulling up in my driveway or walking through my yard, wild animals are highly sensitive to trespassers. During one scouting trip at a beaver pond on Phil's property, I saw the biggest beaver hut I'd ever seen. It was probably thirty feet tall! It wasn't a very cool day, and I was kind of hot from all the walking. For whatever reason, I decided I was going to crawl into the beaver hut to see what was inside of it. I started trying to nudge my way into a bunch of different holes in the beaver dam, and I finally found one that was big enough for me on the back side of it. I was amazed at how the inside of the beaver hut looked. Compared to the chaos on the outside, it was like it was furnished on the inside.

As I was breaking limbs, punching holes, and digging into it, I heard something growling! I turned around and there was a thirty-pound beaver standing about three feet from me. It was on its hind legs in the kill position. I remember thinking, *Man, I've got to get out of here!* Fortunately, I escaped from the beaver before it could get its teeth into me. It was one of the dumbest things I've ever done.

A couple of years later, I found out an angry hog is even worse than an angry beaver. My buddy Mike Williams invited me to go hog-hunting with him on a cantaloupe farm. Wild boars were destroying the cantaloupe crop, and the Louisiana Department of Wildlife and Fisheries gave the landowner permission to have hunters kill the hogs. They even let us chase the boars and shoot them from the back of a truck while the game wardens watched the proceedings from a distance! Now, I'd never hunted hogs, but a few of the guys I was hunting with claimed they were experts. We shot one or two hogs apiece and then chased a 360-pound boar into an adjoining cotton field.

My buddies convinced me to go into the overgrown cotton field and attempt to flush the hog out into the open. About a hundred yards into the thick brush, I heard the hog grunt. The hog was so close to me that when I put my scope on it to shoot, I couldn't tell if it was its front end or rear end! I fired my gun. Unfortunately, I shot the hog in the rear, which only made it madder! The hog turned around and charged toward me. I turned and ran out of the cotton field. I felt its tusks clipping at my ankles as I ran. Fortunately, I stayed ahead of the hog until we reached the cantaloupe field, and then to my surprise the hog fell into a heap. It was dead. I looked at my buddies and they were laughing and rolling on the ground. I thought it was a very strange response to my almost getting devoured by a vicious wild hog. I didn't know I'd lost control of my bladder during the chase!

In my opinion, one of the most frightening verses in the Bible is 1 Peter 5:8, which says: "Be self-controlled and alert. Your enemy the devil prowls around like a roaring lion looking for someone to devour." As a hunter, I can imagine nothing worse than trying to take on a lion. For whatever reason, people tend to view the "evil one" as a fictional character dressed in red with a pitchfork. That type of description of Satan doesn't come from the Bible. John 8:44 describes the devil this way: "He was a murderer from the beginning, not holding to the truth, for there is no truth in him. When he lies, he speaks his native language, for he is a liar and the father of lies." Revelation 12:9–10 depicts Satan as an evil spiritual being that "leads the whole world astray. He was hurled to the earth, and his angels with him."

I think everyone will agree that there is evil in the world. The good news is that Christ defeated all aspects of fear, death, and evil by His death on a cross and triumph over the grave.

Hebrews 2:14–15 says: "Since the children have flesh and blood, he too shared in their humanity so that by his death he might destroy him who holds the power of death—that is, the devil—and free those who all their lives were held in slavery by their fear of death."

The evil one uses camouflage and temptation to lure his prey. But Christ defeated the evil one, and as we surrender to Christ we are safe from being devoured by evil against our will.

As a hunter, I'm aware of how powerful the use of deception and camouflage can be. It's surprising that the evil one's tactics are usually veiled in righteousness. Second Corinthians 11:14 states: "And no wonder, for Satan himself masquerades as an angel of light." The best lie is the one with the most truth, and Satan is the master of using the truth to disguise evil. Even a broken clock is right twice a day! The evil one uses human selfishness as his weapon and offers up a steady dose of pride, pain, and pleasure to keep us from putting our faith and trust in God. First Corinthians 10:13 states: "No temptation has seized you except what is common to man. And God is faithful; he will not let you be tempted beyond what you can bear. But when you are tempted, he will also provide a way out so that you can stand up under it."

> The best lie is the one with the most truth, and Satan is the master of using the truth to disguise evil.

God always provides Christians an escape from any dangerous situation, which is more than I can say for the ducks we lure into our decoys. God overcame a lion by becoming a lamb and giving Himself over to death so that we may live a life free of fear. Our job is to keep our focus on the Creator and enjoy the "created things" from the right perspective.

When dealing with any enemy to our faith in Christ, my favorite passage of scripture is 1 John 4:4, which states: "You, dear children, are from God and have overcome them, because the one who is in you is greater than the one who is in the world."

13

SPRING CLEANING

GETTING READY FOR THE HUNT

*For where you have envy and selfish ambition, there
you find disorder and every evil practice.*

—JAMES 3:16

Growing up on the Ouachita River meant that our lifestyle changed with the fluctuation of the river. We often had to park our vehicles far from our house and then boat up to the front door. One of the reasons my parents were able to purchase two houses and seven acres for such little money—I think they paid twenty-six thousand dollars for the entire property—was that the land was located in a flood zone. My dad actually embraced the Realtor's disclosure with excitement.

The good thing about the flooding was that it was great for the fish spawning in the springtime, and it offered new territories to duck-hunt in the winter. But the bad thing was that our material possessions often broke free and floated downriver. We took turns as lookouts for anything of worth floating downstream. People who live in flood zones are nicknamed "river rats," and I think it's because they have to act a bit like rats during high water.

When the water rose on the Ouachita River, creatures without fins and gills climbed to higher ground, and the first place they seemed to go was our houses. The culprits that caused us the most misery were ants, rats, and snakes. One particular day, when I was only a kid, I heard shotgun blasts near my grandmother's house, and I went next door to investigate. Then another shot rang out! I looked a little more closely and saw a big fish snake in the water, and whoever was shooting at it had done so with a surgical strike. As my grandparents' porch came into view, I saw that my grandmother was the one doing the shooting! She chuckled and asked me, "Did you see that shot?" I couldn't help thinking that maybe the reason my dad is such a good shot had something to do with what I'd just witnessed.

As I said earlier, some of the best memories of my childhood occurred in my grandparents' house. It was extremely upsetting when a great flood in 1991 destroyed their house and everything that was in it. My parents' house was also badly damaged, and I saw firsthand the power and destruction of rapidly rising water. We had to bulldoze the remains of my grandparents' house, but my parents were able to replace their floors and remodel their house. My parents live in that same house to this day, and it's where my entire family gathers for meals on frequent occasions, as some of you have probably seen on episodes of *Duck Dynasty*.

During the flood of 1991, a great friend of mine, W. E. Phillips, and I fished the ditches and bridges of a major highway while the water rose. One of the positives of a flood is that fish swim up with the rising water to feed on the fresh food sources and can be caught like no other time. Fish will gather up at drop-offs and humps during the flood to ambush bait fish. A perfect example of a drop-off where fish gather is a roadside ditch.

One day, W. E. and I parked on the side of the highway and launched our boat in a ditch. Our fishing spot of choice that day was a bubbling culvert right under a fifty-five-mile-per-hour-speed-limit sign. When we started fishing at daylight, there was normal traffic on the road. But as the day went on, water came crashing over low points of the road and traffic stopped when the road was closed. We had set a goal of catching fifty-five large-mouth bass under that sign, and we were paying more attention to reaching our goal than the rising floodwaters. As you have probably already realized, determination is a Robertson trait that is an asset most of the time. But this time, not so much!

> Determination is a Robertson trait that is an asset most of the time. But this time, not so much!

By the time we caught the fifty-five fish and returned to our truck, there was no sign of the road. The current from the water was so strong that our truck was shaking. I quickly realized we had underestimated the speed of the rising water and were now in a dangerous situation. I decided to get in the back of the truck with a life jacket on, while W. E. tried to navigate the submerged road. I had a better vantage point to see the painted lines of the highway, so every time he strayed from the road I banged on the roof of the truck. We traveled about a mile to a bridge on higher ground, where hundreds of people—along with the police—had gathered to watch the spectacle of the flood. I'm positive that we must have looked like Jesus walking on water. Noah might have used a giant ark to escape danger, but we used a truck and some redneck ingenuity! The crowd's faces were filled with shock and bewilderment as they parted to make way for us. At some point, the people started cheering, and I felt like a politician running for office as I waved to the crowd. Even though we were basking in the glory of the moment and had an ice chest full of fish, we realized we were very fortunate to have survived.

Another positive thing to come out of the floods was that the higher water levels revealed the areas on my dad's property that ducks liked, and we took note of where they gathered. During high water, we also floated huge cypress logs to duck holes and used them to build duck blinds on. The high waters gave us access to lakes full of logs that we otherwise wouldn't have had access to. After the floods receded, we had permanent blinds in spots where we knew ducks preferred to go. Over the years, my dad also purchased some of the adjoining land where we saw ducks during floods. By using the watermarks on the trees as a guide, we built levees and water-control structures to simulate the habitat that ducks seemed to favor.

Before my dad purchased the additional property, we leased land at a hunting club in Tensas Parish, which is about eighty miles from our home. The land was located near the Mississippi River and was a great place to shoot ducks. My dad has always had a love affair with cypress tree breaks because of their beauty and the fact that ducks really seem to like what they have to offer. The trees provide a resting spot for ducks and usually have waist-deep water and green seed for them to eat.

My dad was part of the lease in Tensas Parish for a couple of years, and in the second year, when I was about thirteen, we were involved in a major flood. My dad guided hunts to help pay for the cost of his share of the lease and to make extra money. As a kid in school, I saved my sick days for duck-hunting season. Under Louisiana laws, we were given twenty unexcused absences every academic year. Even if I was sick with a high fever or stomach virus before hunting season, I went to school so I could save my sick days to go duck-hunting. But as soon as cold fronts came down during hunting season, I became afflicted with what I called "duck fever." The school I attended later implemented the "Jase Rule," which required a doctor's excuse for days missed, which I find kind of sad.

During the year of the flood, I remember begging my dad to take me to Tensas Parish because of an approaching cold front. I knew the ducks would be coming there with it. My dad took me along mainly as a camp helper because he'd booked a full group of out-of-town hunters. Our camp was an old trailer sitting on a hump in the middle of a field beside the cypress break. Because the river was rising, the field became a safe haven for mice and ants. Every critter that crawls on the ground either drowns or moves to higher ground when water rises. The problem was our camp was on the highest point of ground for miles! My primary job was to kill the mice. My dad brought a dozen spring traps to catch them.

I'll never forget when we walked into the trailer. I saw mice scampering in every direction. There also was a man staying at the trailer who had helped my dad guide a previous trip. His name was Wayne, and he was from Missouri. He had decided to remain at the camp and become the caretaker while my dad was away. I'm not sure if it was because of the mice, the isolation, or a combination of both, but he seemed a little bit bewildered when I met him. He had actually frightened the wife of one of the other men who leased the property. When she showed up at the camp unannounced, Wayne believed she was an angel in a dream who had been sent to save him.

As I started to set out the traps, one would pop before the next one was set. I caught over two hundred mice the first night! As I went to bed that night, I could hardly sleep from the anticipation of the next day's hunt. I'd persuaded my dad to put me in a tree blind by myself while he entertained the out-of-town hunters in another tree blind about five hundred yards away. I also couldn't sleep because I heard mice scurrying all over the trailer.

As I finally started to close my eyes, I heard quite a commotion from my dad, who was sleeping in a bunk below me. Then I heard a loud thud against the wall.

"Danged rat was trying to build a nest in my beard," he said. "He needs to find somewhere else to build a nest."

My dad and I started laughing.

"We're going to need some more mousetraps, Jase," he said.

My dad finally decided to kill the mice with poison, which drove them to a leaky hot water tank. The line of mice trekking to the water tank turned into a traffic jam inside the walls of the trailer. When the lead mice died, those coming behind crowded into one another, dying in heaps—and then the ants started eating them. When we looked inside the walls, the dead mice were stacked like bricks. There were hundreds of them, and they looked like insulation.

As the week went on, the smell of the dead mice became so bad that it eventually ran us out of the trailer. Phil decided he would one day burn the trailer and start over at the camp. Ultimately, the state took over the property and turned it into a wildlife refuge, so we lost the lease, too. It became a burial ground for one of the greatest mouse infestations in human history. It was epic.

Unfortunately, mice are the least of our worries when we're cleaning out our duck blinds before hunting season. We've found all kinds of wildlife in our blinds—mostly snakes, insects, alligators, and birds. We were spring-cleaning one of our blinds and stumbled upon four baby birds in a nest built in our coffeepot. They were small yellow-breasted birds that are known as great crested flycatchers. We decided to help them along, and after a few days of observation and feeding, they flew away healthy. To some it might seem ironic that we would help raise birds in a place where we shoot ducks, but it is a principle of what we do as hunters. We spend way more time, energy, and money helping the future population of ducks and their habitat than we do shooting a few for supper during hunting season. There has never been a single duck season in which hunters shot even 1 percent of the number of ducks that died during the migration process. Humans have a responsibility to keep the animal kingdom balanced, and hunters are the primary caretakers of animals' habitats and their future well-being.

Back to my story about the trip with my dad to the flooded Tensas Parish and his promise to put me in a duck blind by myself while he conducted his guided hunt. My dad dropped me off at the tree blind—which was about thirty feet up a tree—before daylight. I was beginning to experiment with duck calls for the first time. I had a knack for it. My dad says it takes about a year for the average person to learn how to blow a duck call, but I listened to him talk to other people about how to do it. Of course, I also listened to him blow duck calls, and there wasn't anyone better I could have learned from. I never tried to blow a duck call until I had all the required information, and then I went out and tried it with real ducks. I'd listen to them, and then I'd blow. I'd listen again, and then I'd blow.

> We spend way more time, energy, and money helping the future population of ducks and their habitat than we do shooting a few for supper during hunting season.

On that morning at Tensas Parish, a cold front passed through, and it was about thirty degrees with a strong north wind. As the boat full of my dad's hunting party puttered away into darkness, I quickly realized I wasn't wearing enough clothes to stay warm.

I was wearing two layers: pants, a shirt, and a pair of coveralls. I started pacing up and down the duck blind to keep my blood circulating. After several minutes, the sun was a welcome sight, because I figured it would start to warm up. Unfortunately, it didn't get much warmer.

Before too long, I saw a few ducks fly close by. I was under strict orders from my dad to only shoot ducks that I called in over my decoys. I was sending out an occasional call but wasn't getting a response. Then I'd hear volleys of gunfire from my dad's blind, which caused me to jump. I realized then that the only thing worse than being in the wrong spot was being close enough to hear someone else in the right spot!

By midmorning, my excitement and anticipation had turned into complete misery because of the cold. But all of a sudden two mallard ducks flew by me at eye level. I grabbed my duck call and blew on it about three times. The ducks stopped, turned, floated down, and sat in the decoy spread in front of me. I grabbed my gun, but my body was so cold that I couldn't raise it to my shoulder. Actually, I was even colder than before, because when nature called, I was forced to unzip my coveralls. When I was finished doing my business, my fingers were too numb to zip the coveralls back up!

Despite not being able to shoot, I felt a great sense of pride and accomplishment as I reflected on calling in wild ducks for the first time. It was amazing to me that the ducks were swimming around painted decoys because of the sounds I made with a call. I was instantly hooked and it really didn't matter to me that I was too cold to shoot. Unfortunately, my dad pulled up to my blind in his boat about the same time. He watched the ducks fly away from my decoys. He pointed at them in amazement.

"Why didn't you shoot?" he asked me.

Due to my pride, I decided to tell him, "I didn't want to mess y'all up with my gunfire."

My dad shook his head in disbelief.

"But I called them in with these duck calls I made," I proudly told him.

The next day, I went into my dad's shop, where he was boring barrels for duck calls.

"Hey, you want to hear my duck call?" I asked him. I was a little bit nervous because I'd never blown a call in front of him before.

"Yeah, let me he hear it," he said.

I blew on the duck call.

"You sound like a gadwall," he said.

A gadwall hen sounds like a mallard hen, except her cadence is a little shorter and sounds scratchier. But they're pretty close. I didn't know if he was complimenting me or criticizing me!

"Hey, look on the bright side," he said. "If the sperm count had been lower, you might have come out as a shoveler."

Shovelers are pretty much trash ducks and aren't very good to eat. But after Phil told me I sounded like a gadwall, I've always had a special place for them in my heart. Several years later, I actually invented the first gadwall drake call. Gadwalls are unique in that the hen very rarely makes a sound. One day, we were working the ducks, and I had a mallard hen call in one hand and our six-in-one whistle in the other because we were working pintails. I blew the hen call and then the whistle. One time, I blew them at the same time and stopped. *That sounds like a gadwall drake,* I thought to myself. I started blowing them simultaneously so my dad could hear them.

"Hey, you might be onto something," he said. "Why don't we try that? We'll get the gadwall decoys and try it on 'em. If it gets them into the decoys, we'll figure out a way to build them."

It was amazing how many gadwalls responded to my drake call. We ended up building the call, and no one has successfully duplicated it. It isn't the prettiest of duck calls, but it's effective.

My first attempt at making duck calls was through trial and error, before I'd even attempted to call in ducks on my own. Of course, my dad invented wooden duck calls that were the first double-reeded calls in the world. The most critical component of a duck call is the insert or soundboard where the reeds sit. To my knowledge, my dad was the first person to successfully mass-produce duck calls made with cedar inserts. Cedar is a soft wood and once you start boring holes into it, it's an imperfect system because the wood gives way sporadically. That's what makes every duck call an original. They are dependent on the skill of a call maker to reach their full potential. There really aren't two of them alike. We've made tens of thousands of wooden calls through the years,

> "You might be onto something," Phil told me. "If it gets the gadwalls into the decoys, we'll figure out a way to build them."

and not two of them sound identical. Each call seems like a new creation crafted with its own uniqueness.

Duck calls remind me of how God uses people to make Himself known. Like duck calls, people are all a bit different and are dependent on their maker and designer for their individualism in life. Duck calls and their unique individual sounds breathe life into decoys that are essentially dead. Likewise, God uses different people with unique perspectives to illustrate His existence and shout out the message of eternal life through Jesus Christ. The audible sound that each mallard hen makes is virtually the same; however, the tone and cadence are unique. Similarly, the Gospel message is the same yesterday, today, and forever, yet the perspective and life experience are different and unique for each person relaying it.

We Duckmen have always been on a mission to build the world's greatest duck blind. The largest blind we ever built is on my dad's property, and it is named the Lake Blind. It has three sides of shooting porches with a fully functional kitchen and living quarters in the middle. The side that does not have a shooting porch functions as a pull-in garage for the boat. The blind has a stove, a refrigerator, bunk beds, and a commode. We put the toilet in because once we had a guest relieve himself at the entrance of the blind, but he missed his mark a bit, leaving his waste products on the blind itself! My dad was not happy, so the next thing we knew we had a toilet—complete with plumbing that was battery operated! The blind is awesome, especially on slow days, but it is a haven for everything that roams the swamp.

One time, one of the guys hunting with us climbed into a sleeping bag on one of the bunks to take a nap. He didn't know there was a nest of black-faced bees in his bag! He was stung all over his body. It was a two-day ordeal getting the bees and sleeping bag out of the blind. Phil had to wrap his entire body and wear a mask to get them out. I was decked out in football gear, complete with shoulder pads and a helmet. The only places I did not have completely covered were my eyes and nose. In spite of my efforts, I was stung right between the eyes and couldn't see for two days due to the swelling.

One of our most dangerous missions before hunting season is de-snaking our blinds. Because of the location of most of our blinds, they're a hot spot for cottonmouth moccasins and other venomous snakes. During one cleaning we killed a couple of cottonmouths and a black widow spider. Phil walked out onto the shooting porch and said, "I think we got it." As I looked at Phil, I saw a cottonmouth hanging from a button willow only inches from his head. After prompting my dad to duck, I shot the snake over his head.

We built another duck blind on floating cypress logs at a beaver pond on Phil's property. As I climbed out of the duck blind one day to retrieve some ducks, I stepped on a log with a hole in it. I didn't know there was a cottonmouth moccasin inside the hole! When I came back, I stepped on the log again and the snake struck at my face. I leaped back and fell into the water. It was the closest encounter I have ever had, and after the near miss, I retaliated with my shotgun and killed the snake. When you're in the woods or swamp, if you get bit by a venomous snake, your chances of surviving are slim because you're so far away from a hospital and antivenin. It's one of the biggest dangers of hunting, but it's a risk we're willing to take. It's amazing none of us has ever been bitten.

At the time of this writing, we have around forty duck blinds on my dad's property. It is a full-time job maintaining the blinds in the off-season, and oftentimes some of the blinds are forgotten until ducks start going into their areas.

A couple of years ago, we were hunting an old blind that was literally falling apart. One of our cameramen noticed a jar sitting inside a huge crack in the floor. He retrieved the jar and saw that it was full of brown fuzzy pickles—with an expiration date eleven years old! His discovery began a very entertaining debate about the health hazards of eating one of the pickles, which we assumed had once been green. Phil and I believed eating one would make you sick for at least a couple of days. Uncle Si thought their consumption would cause immediate death. However, the cameraman, who has a degree in microbiology, gave a long list of reasons why the twelve-year-old pickles were fit for human consumption. He ate one of the pickles, despite the gags and gasps of everyone watching, including Uncle Si's exclamations for someone to call 911! The cameraman never showed any signs of discomfort, even though he did admit it tasted awful. This is one of the many reasons my dad has always described cameramen as "weirdos."

The strangest thing we've found in our blinds during our annual cleanings was a female buzzard, which had built a nest and laid an egg in the middle of one of our tree blinds. The smell was indescribable and produced an immediate gag reflex. In an effort to relocate the buzzard, I discovered the hard way that an angry buzzard's best defense is projectile vomiting. We eventually removed the buzzard, but we couldn't do anything about the smell. We tried everything known to man to get rid of it, but nothing worked. We determined that we couldn't cohabitate with a buzzard and eventually burned the blind and started over.

The incident with the buzzard reminds me so much of our spiritual well-being. As a Christian, there are some situations you can't reside in and stay faithful to Christ. Second Peter 2:22 describes the problem of not breaking free from your past lifestyle and declaring Jesus Christ as Lord: "Of them the proverbs are true: 'A dog returns to its vomit' and, 'A sow that is washed goes back to her wallowing in the mud.'"

Real buzzards were made by God for the specific purpose of feeding on rotten things, but from a spiritual perspective, who wants a buzzard-type lifestyle? As a human, if you feed on evil, rotten things,

> I discovered the hard way that an angry buzzard's best defense is projectile vomiting.

your spiritual lifestyle will stink. And just like the buzzard defends its domain with projectile vomiting, people spew filth from their mouth toward Christians when their evil behavior is threatened. First Peter 4:3–4 states: "For you have spent enough time in the past doing what pagans choose to do—living in debauchery, lust, drunkenness, orgies, carousing and detestable idolatry. They think it strange that you do not plunge with them into the same flood of dissipation, and they heap abuse on you." In a world flooded with dissipation, Jesus Christ is always the high ground.

The best way to keep a duck blind free of unwelcome guests is to make use of it through hunting. A potential nuisance runs from gunfire, never toward it. It is the same for our spiritual lives. A good friend of mine, Charlie Murray, who went on to be with the Lord a few years ago, told me once, "We should live for God out loud and on purpose, instead of hunkered down in a church building." By unselfishly proclaiming Christ, your mind is not programmed to please yourself, and this eases the burden of temptations. James 3:16 says, "For where you have envy and selfish ambition, there you find disorder and every evil practice." When Christ was on the earth, He was focused on introducing people to God, and by doing that He was void of doing anything wrong. Sharing the message of Jesus is a proven recipe for overcoming sin in our life. I have noticed that when you are bold about your faith, people tend to join you or run from you. Most people find it difficult to be bold because their past has given them a reputation that keeps them silent about their faith, even if they want the benefits of a life in Christ. Fortunately, God provides a way to start over.

Surrendering yourself to Christ through baptism is God's way of ridding a person of his or her past evil actions, and He replaces your past with His Spirit, which enables us to lead others to Christ. It is interesting that Peter compared baptism in Christ to the waters that flooded the earth in Noah's day. First Peter 3:20–21 states: "God waited patiently in the days of Noah while the ark was being built. In it only a few people, eight in all, were saved through water, and this water symbolizes baptism that now saves you also—not the removal of dirt from the body but the pledge of a good conscience toward God. It saves you by the resurrection of Jesus Christ." There is nothing holy about the water itself. Baptism is a privilege offered by God to participate in the death, burial, and resurrection of Christ.

Evaluate your life and determine if you are influencing others for good or being influenced by evil. There is no middle ground. Matthew 24:28 states: "Wherever there is a carcass, there the vultures will gather." Who are you running with? What does your lifestyle smell like? Matthew 22:32 says this about the almighty God: "He is not the God of the dead but of the living." There comes a time in life when we need to bury the past and start over, and that is what Jesus Christ is all about. He died so that we might live; He lives so that we might die only to live for Him.

14

---·•·---

HUNTING IN HEAVEN

LOOKING TO THE FUTURE

But our citizenship is in heaven. And we eagerly await
a Savior from there, the Lord Jesus Christ, who, by the
power that enables him to bring everything under his
control, will transform our lowly bodies so that they
will be like his glorious body.

—PHILIPPIANS 3:20

In December 2012, the Washington Nationals first baseman
Adam LaRoche, who has become one of my good friends, asked
me to come and share the message of Christ at the community
center in his hometown of Fort Scott, Kansas. A few days before
I was scheduled to speak, Adam sent me a text message and asked
me, "Do you think there's hunting in heaven?" Now, my dad likes
to joke that heaven to him is thousands of miles of marshlands
and cypress breaks without a game warden (or any kind of concrete) in sight!

To be honest, I really am not concerned about what it looks like or what we are going to do. Personally, I believe that just making it to heaven should be our primary concern. I have always viewed heaven as part of the journey toward eternity with other people, angels, and God. However, I told Adam I believe hunting is possible in heaven, based on what I've read and studied in the Bible.

After Jesus emerged from his tomb as a resurrected being, He appeared to His disciples near the Sea of Galilee, though His disciples didn't recognize Him at first. In John 21:6 Jesus said, "Throw your net on the right side of the boat and you will find some." His disciples had been unable to catch fish the night before, but Jesus led them to 153 fish that morning without one torn mesh of the net (as a former commercial fisherman, I can attest that that is quite a feat). The disciples eventually realized it was Jesus, and in John 21:12 He said to them, "Come and have breakfast." This resurrected Christ organized and participated in the consumption of two of the five food groups (fish of the sea and bread) as described in Genesis 9:2–3. Why did He do that? Jesus wasn't eating fish and bread to stay alive—He was now imperishable.

You need to remember that all of Jesus' disciples believed He was dead. They were still consumed with pain, grief, and the shame that they had turned their backs on Him. They hadn't recognized Him as Lord when He hung on the cross. However, their eyes were opened at a fish fry as they gathered around a campfire on the shore. Death did not deter their conversation. They looked into the eyes of their friend, brother, and resurrected Lord. It is no wonder that every one of those men at the fish fry would eventually surrender his life to an awful, torturous death rather than deny his Lord and Savior. There is something to be said about gathering around a dinner table to eat a meal with those you love while sharing, laughing (sometimes crying), and praying together to a God who believes in a forever family.

One of the best things about working at Duck Commander over the years has been meeting so many of our fans at trade shows and other events around the country. It's really uplifting to meet other duck hunters and hear their stories about hunting and faith in God. It always makes me proud to learn that people associate my family with Jesus and that we've had a positive impact on so many. It reminds me that the Lord is using us to spread His message to whomever we can. Some of the people we've met on the road have become our lifelong friends, and some of the stories we've heard have left lasting impressions.

A few years ago, my dad and I met a couple during a trade show in Memphis. We were selling our duck calls and hunting DVDs, and the couple approached us and told us about their son. They said he was a big fan of Duck Commander and was in the hospital battling cancer. They told us his prognosis wasn't good and asked us to pray for him. Such encounters are not uncommon for us. My dad said, "I'll do better than that. Take me to the hospital." It was not a typical response from him. Obviously, we can't go to the hospital bed of each person who asks us to pray for him or her; however, my dad seemed led to do it that time. My dad prayed with the young man and made a deal with him.

"I'll tell you what," my dad said. "If the Almighty heals you, and you get back on your feet, I'll take you duck-hunting with us."

We've had many prayers through the years with people in similar circumstances. Sometimes in life, all you can do is pray. Most of the time, we leave and are left only to wonder what happened. In this particular case, we were at the same trade show in Memphis the next year, and a young man with a full head of hair and shaggy beard approached us. He had a calendar under his arm.

> "I'll tell you what," my dad said. "If the Almighty heals you, and you get back on your feet, I'll take you duck-hunting with us."

"Remember me?" he asked my dad.

Of course, my dad didn't immediately recognize him because he looked so different. But after the man explained he was the guy from the hospital, my dad realized why he was there.

"Oh, yeah," my dad said. "You're going to hold me to that duck hunt."

When duck season came later that year, the guy and his father traveled to West Monroe, Louisiana, to go duck-hunting with us. The hunt was during a driving rainstorm, so the ducks were very much on the move. Despite the bad weather, it was one of those hunts in which you could barely keep your gun loaded because the action was so fierce. Everyone was soaked from the rain, but we were smiling from ear to ear. Immediately after our new friend shot the last duck to meet our limit, the rain stopped, and one of the most spectacular rainbows I've ever seen appeared in the sky.

My dad said a prayer, offering the Almighty thanks for the day, the abundance of ducks, and the presence of our guests.

As I drove the man and his father back to my parents' house for breakfast after the hunt, the guy asked me, "Was that a normal hunt?" I'm pretty sure he was referring to the number of ducks we shot, but his question seemed to overwhelm all of us with emotion.

"We shot our limit of ducks in less than an hour, saw the most awesome rainbow, and did it with a man who defied the medical diagnosis and was given up for dead," I said.

In retrospect, there wasn't anything normal about the hunt. As it says in Matthew 19:26, one of my favorite Bible verses, "Jesus looked at them and said, 'With man this is impossible, but with God all things are possible.'" Certainly, the abnormal is sometimes normal for those who believe in Him. That particular day in the blind with the young man who battled cancer and won became known as the "Rainbow Hunt," and it made a lasting impression in my life.

More than anything, it was further evidence to me that God is in control. Romans 8:38 says: "For I am convinced that neither death nor life, neither angels nor demons, neither the present nor the future, nor any powers, neither height nor depth, nor anything else in all creation, will be able to separate us from the love of God that is in Christ Jesus our Lord." Whatever your views are about Jesus, the Bible, religion, or life in general, we can agree that life is a gift; we did not choose to be here. My belief system does not come from a religious denomination or creed. It comes from the Bible. By having heard its message, I was led to its Author, whom I believe is our Maker, universe Designer, and ultimately our Savior.

Romans 10:17 says: "Consequently, faith comes from hearing the message, and the message is heard through the word about Christ." God provides everyone on our planet a reference manual through His Bible. God reveals Himself through the Bible and unleashes a power that is difficult to explain. This power can be clearly seen in the changed lives of people who come to an understanding of the message. I witnessed the transformation in my parents, and it was extremely influential in my life. For generations, the Bible has changed the vilest hearts into positive role models and has been evidence of the existence of an almighty God.

> Whatever your views are about Jesus, the Bible, religion, or life in general, we can agree that life is a gift.

As I said earlier, my first thoughts about God came in a duck blind as I gazed upon the diversity and beauty of creation. There is nothing in nature that can be reproduced or equaled by humans. None of our computers, microchips, or cell phones can duplicate what God has put forth. Viewing the details of this magnificent earth is better than any sermon from any preacher I have heard about the evidence of God.

Jim McGuiggan, a preacher from Ireland, probably had the most influence on me in a formal teaching setting. Outside of my family, my wife, my kids, the Bible, and God Himself, I've probably learned more from him than anyone else I've ever heard.

What's ironic is that I have nothing in common with him, besides our faith in Christ. I can barely understand a word he says because he speaks with such a strong Irish accent, and I'm sure I'd sound funny to him if he ever heard me speak.

The one thing Mr. McGuiggan taught me is that the Bible is a compilation of letters written throughout human history by a living God. The love letters God wrote are special because they lead us to a relationship with an actual being. It's hard to believe—but it's true—that an all-powerful God wants to live in loving fellowship with all men. I remember hearing Mr. McGuiggan use an illustration of marriage to show the necessity of having a relationship with God. He made a point that the only reason a love letter is special to people is because of the bond shared with the one who wrote it. If someone's wife carried around letters from her husband, even sang songs about him, had weekly suppers in his name, and told others about him, but never had an actual relationship with him, the moments of honor would not be special at all.

As Psalm 136:5–9 tell us, creation was God's power expressed in love. By reading and understanding the Bible as a series of love letters to men and women, you begin to recognize the tender and mighty love of God. The Bible is not a rule book for life or a collection of fairy tales; it's a weapon of mass instruction. It's a love letter from God to humanity. It's an introduction to Jesus Christ, who is God in human form. It declares to the world: God is for you, not against you. To me, the Bible is a work of nonfiction broken into three parts: from Genesis to Malachi, it's about Jesus

Christ coming to earth; from Matthew to John, it's about Jesus' life on earth; and from Acts to Revelation, it's about Jesus coming back to earth. It's all about Jesus and how we can have a relationship with the omnipotent, omnipresent, omniscient, eternal, holy, and righteous Almighty. This relationship is more important than simply joining a church or doing a few good things.

For me, a lot of answers to life's questions can be found in Acts 17:22–28. When Paul was in Athens, Greece, he was distressed to find a city full of false idols. As he stood in front of a meeting of the Areopagus, the Greek high court, he told them, "The God who made the world and everything in it is the Lord of heaven and earth and does not live in temples built by hands.

> The Bible is not a rule book for life or a collection of fairy tales; it's a love letter from God to humanity.

And he is not served by human hands, as if he needed anything, because he himself gives all men life and breath and everything else."

To imagine a God who created a world full of individuals who are profoundly different and all loved by Him boggles the mind yet brings hope and clarity to our souls. If God has created you purposely and out of love, then your life is not an accident. All people have the same origin, and as the scripture above says, we all have the same father, despite our differing DNA. I realize that believing God made all races from one man might seem implausible to some, but the idea that we evolved from single cells—or that humanity came from thin air—requires too much faith for me and offers nothing in the area of hope. I believe we are masterpieces made by God on purpose, with a purpose beyond simply existing. His authority as Creator was validated when His Son overcame the finality of death.

Whenever I meet somebody—religious or not—I start right there, with Jesus' power over death. Like I did with my buddies in high school, when I was only beginning to become vocal about my faith, I ask people three questions: How did you get on the earth? (I believe God made you.) What are you supposed to be doing here? (You're supposed to find and have a relationship with God, who made you.) And, finally, how are you leaving the earth? (Jesus left the earth flying without mechanical aid because gravity no longer had an effect on His resurrected body.)

One of the most frequently asked questions I get from non-believers is "How do you know the Bible is true?" Second Peter 1:16–21 gives us this response: "We did not follow cleverly invented stories when we told you about the coming of our Lord Jesus Christ, but we were eyewitnesses of his majesty. . . . For prophecy never had its origin in the will of man, but men spoke from God as they were carried along by the Holy Spirit."

Ultimately, no one can verify the events written more than two thousand years ago because time machines do not exist. We are left with documentation, evidence, common sense, and faith. Hebrews 11:1 says: "Now faith is being sure of what we hope for and certain of what we do not see."

Perhaps the best evidence for the existence and validity of Jesus Christ as God in flesh is found in history books document-ing the deaths of His closest followers and disciples. After Jesus' resurrection, nearly all of His closest followers and apostles were martyred because of their refusal to deny Christ's resurrection. If they hadn't seen the resurrected Lord, I can't believe they would have been willing to die to defend Him. Who would die for a lie knowing it was a lie? Most of their deaths are not found in the Bible, but historical accounts offer some grisly details of the manner in which they died because of their belief in Christ. If they had only said, "It was a hoax," their lives would have been spared.

Hebrews 7:16 reveals the true reason Jesus is the priest and mediator between mankind and God and why He is Lord: He is "one who has become a priest not on the basis of a regulation as to his ancestry but on the basis of the power of an indestructible life." If someone were truly indestructible, then those who belong to him would have a secure future and a reason to smile, even in the face of death. Jesus Christ is the sole leader of a major movement of people that began to flourish only after He died. Of course, He came back from the dead no longer able to die again. That is someone who deserves to be followed by mass quantities of people.

Who would die for a lie knowing it was a lie?

The hope for our own resurrection comes from the same power displayed by Christ when he conquered death. Philippians 3:20 says: "But our citizenship is in heaven. And we eagerly await a Savior from there, the Lord Jesus Christ, who, by the power that enables him to bring everything under his control, will transform our lowly bodies so that they will be like his glorious body." The body that Christ currently inhabits is immortal, imperishable, indestructible, and capable of enjoying a fish fry. First Corinthians 15:54 says: "When the perishable has been clothed with the imperishable, and the mortal with immortality, then the saying that is written will come true: 'Death has been swallowed up in victory.'"

In essence, when a person hears that message and accepts Christ as Lord, and reenacts His death, burial, and resurrection in baptism, he or she then receives God's Spirit, which is the same Spirit that resurrected His Son and will resurrect us. The fruits of His Spirit are love, joy, peace, patience, goodness, faithfulness, self-control, and all other good things. Goodness comes from God's Spirit because we're flawed and make mistakes, which the cross took care of and through which we have a second chance. Today, Jesus Christ is still alive and well in heaven and represents those of us on earth who follow Him. Christ's actions after His resurrection are chronicled in Acts 1:3–10. He stayed on earth for forty days, giving many convincing proofs that He was alive, before ascending to heaven, where He now acts as mediator between God and those who trust Him.

One of my good friends, Randy Kirby, told me one time that you should wake up every morning thinking about the cross, because it gives you the ability to start over again and forgive others. And then you should go to bed every night thinking about the resurrection, because no matter what happens in the end, you have hope of living again. The part in between is where God uses us to represent Him on earth. Christ has forgiven our past and secured our future, which enables us to make the most of the present opportunities to bring others to Christ.

GOOD CALL

I make duck calls, but I represent my Maker through what I do to make a living. I've always said that if He can use me, He can use anybody to make known the good news of His Son.

Is there hunting in heaven? I say, "Let's go have breakfast." Of course, the menu wouldn't matter to me, but I would gladly volunteer to obtain 153 fish or even heavenly ducks. I yearn to see my close friends Angel Gist and Charlie Murray, my grandparents, and many members of my family and friends who have passed from this life. It is always sad to lose those you are close to on this earth, and I will have to continue to deal with it unless I go next.

I remember hearing Mr. McGuiggan relate what he deemed a curious story with a powerful message. He told the story of a young boy struggling with worry and grief because he had lost a loved one. The boy had a dream in which he met a flower, to which he declared, "I am scared to die." The flower responded, "I am not, because even though I'm here for only a short time, I will come back next spring more beautiful than before." The boy came across a caterpillar and exclaimed, "I am scared to die!" The caterpillar replied, "I am not, because I shall be transformed into a beautiful butterfly." At last the little boy approached an angel and shouted, "I am scared to die!" The angel retorted, "You are dead!" The thing he feared the most had already happened, and he wasn't even aware of it.

I truly believe the resurrection of Jesus Christ guarantees those who trust Him eternal life free from pain, discomfort, and death. In the end we will win. Whether we are alive or dead when

Jesus returns, we have nothing to worry about. First Thessalonians 4:13–18 describes our final journey, and Paul gives the reason we don't grieve as those without hope: "We believe that Jesus died and rose again and so we believe that God will bring with Jesus those who have fallen asleep in him . . . We who are still alive and are left will be caught up together with them in the clouds to meet the Lord in the air. And so we will be with the Lord forever."

I'm going to enjoy the journey on earth with those around me. As far as what heaven will be like, I'm going to roll with my dad on that one. I hope heaven consists of no concrete, meals together around the table, and no game wardens!

MORE BOOKS FROM YOUR
DUCK DYNASTY® FAVORITES!

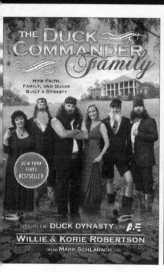

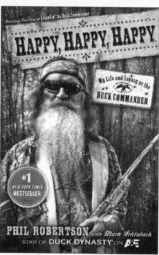

HOWARD BOOKS
A Division of Simon & Schuster
A CBS COMPANY

Printed in the United States
By Bookmasters